Lucinda

You brought
Create the Future
to life!

Nick Williams

PRAISE FOR *CREATE THE FUTURE*

"An inspiring and practical handbook for leaders—from start-ups to mature firms—who must choose the path forward for their company."

—**DEMOS PARNEROS,** FORMER PRESIDENT, STAPLES NORTH AMERICA, AND FORMER CEO, BARNES & NOBLE

"In today's rapidly changing business environment, leaders need to be laser-focused on identifying the right problem and coming up with innovative solutions. Read this book and learn how to imagine your company's future and create the path to success. Along the way, learn how to imagine your future as an authentic and innovative leader—it's a win-win."

—**BILL BURNETT,** COAUTHOR OF *DESIGNING YOUR LIFE* AND *DESIGNING YOUR NEW WORK LIFE* AND EXECUTIVE DIRECTOR OF THE LIFE DESIGN LAB AT STANFORD UNIVERSITY

"Rick Williams brilliantly delivers a leadership compass for high-performing companies. With his wealth of experience, veteran consultant Williams provides a clear playbook that's indispensable for leaders seeking a practical approach to shaping their organization's destiny. Packed with structured team exercises, this book empowers leaders to make choices that resonate with their goals and values. Like an in-house management consultant, *Create the Future* is your invaluable resource for decision-making in turbulent times."

—**HUBERT JOLY,** FORMER CEO, BEST BUY; SENIOR LECTURER, HARVARD BUSINESS SCHOOL; AND AUTHOR OF *THE HEART OF BUSINESS*

"Rick Williams has produced a valuable book that can help leaders make better decisions when thinking strategically about the future of their organizations. *Create the Future* is a book to be read and applied."

—**LT. GEN. H. R. MCMASTER,** FORMER WHITE HOUSE NATIONAL SECURITY ADVISOR AND AUTHOR OF THE *NEW YORK TIMES* BESTSELLER *BATTLEGROUNDS*

"Rick Williams' *Create the Future* is like having your own personal coach to help guide your decisions and create a better future, both professionally and personally. This book gives you the framework to think bolder and act accordingly, so you can manifest your future as you desire. Highly recommended to all leaders of high-performance teams and those who believe that within themselves there is a brighter future ahead."

—**DAVID KAHAN,** PRESIDENT AND CEO, BIRKENSTOCK AMERICAS

"Even the brightest and most experienced leaders among us can fall into the trap of working hard toward 'something' but not knowing exactly what that something is. *Create the Future* shows us the importance and power of clear purposes and clear thinking. This book helps us grapple with the question of where our company should go, from someone who has already been there."

—**DOUG STONE AND SHEILA HEEN,** COAUTHORS OF THE BESTSELLER *DIFFICULT CONVERSATIONS* AND FACULTY IN NEGOTIATION AT HARVARD LAW SCHOOL

"At last, a management book geared for the realities people in business face today. Rick Williams has produced a tremendously wise and practical guide, aptly titled *Create the Future*, for navigating the uncertainty that lies ahead in every industry. His methodology, developed from decades of rarified experience in business, can help anyone who wants to learn how to make and implement better decisions."

—**AMY C. EDMONDSON,** NOVARTIS PROFESSOR OF LEADERSHIP, HARVARD BUSINESS SCHOOL; AUTHOR OF *RIGHT KIND OF WRONG*

"Finally—a book that boils down the decision-making tools of the top corporate consultants into a valuable step-by-step process for taking your organization and yourself from where you are to where you want to be. Whatever challenge you are facing, *Create the Future* can help you overcome it."

—**BOB ADAMS,** FOUNDER, BUSINESSTOWN

"India's Vedanta philosophy has four principles suggested for business and leaders that remain important and relevant even three thousand years after they were written. First, be self-aware. Second, protect the resources that help you. Third, serve others before self. Fourth and last, be decisive but implement with compassion. In the tradition of the Vedanta, *Create the Future* presents a modern version of timeless and valuable principles that are too often forgotten."

—**R. GOPALAKRISHNAN,** BESTSELLING AUTHOR OF
THE CASE OF THE BONSAI MANAGER AND *THE BIOGRAPHY OF INNOVATIONS*

"*Create the Future* is a practical field manual for making the important decisions required to seize an opportunity or address a threat. As a coach, I work with leaders facing difficult challenges. The CTF exercises are an excellent step-by-step guide for taking your organization to the next level without a big consulting fee."

—**BERNHARD HEINE,** FOUNDER, PROFESSIONAL BUSINESS COACHES, INC.

"*Create the Future* provides a unique, disciplined approach with actionable steps that enable a CEO and the leadership team to create their own success."

—**LAWRENCE SIFF,** FOUNDER AND CEO,
NEPTUNE ADVISORS AND C LEVEL COMMUNITY

"It is a joy to experience a book that introduces a useful managerial framework grounded in practical experience and supported by a step-by-step process of intervention and improvement. Reading this book stimulates my desire to seek out opportunities to Create the Future. It will do the same for you!"

—**LEN SCHLESINGER,** BAKER FOUNDATION PROFESSOR,
HARVARD BUSINESS SCHOOL; PRESIDENT EMERITUS AT BABSON COLLEGE

"*Create the Future* masterfully bridges the gap between creativity and strategic decision-making. It is a must-read for leaders who aspire to navigate the complexities of modern business with a blend of innovation and practical wisdom. This book is an essential tool kit for anyone looking to elevate their company without the hefty price tag of external consulting."

—**TONY MARTIGNETTI,** LEADERSHIP ADVISOR; FOUNDER,
INSPIRED PURPOSE PARTNERS; AND BESTSELLING AUTHOR OF
CAMPFIRE LESSONS FOR LEADERS AND *CLIMBING THE RIGHT MOUNTAIN*

"*Create the Future* is an essential book for anyone trying to dramatically change the trajectory of a business. Rick Williams captures the key steps for such transformation clearly and concisely. Extraordinary success often lies at the intersection of deep insights and speed of action. Williams gives us the tools for both."

—**MOHAMAD ALI,** COO, IBM CONSULTING; FORMER CEO OF IDG AND CARBONITE

"Certain to inspire, *Create the Future* is a masterclass in innovative leadership. This book, with its practical insights and transformative strategies, is an essential read for modern leaders. Williams' expertise guides you from establishing a visionary mindset to executing impactful decisions. A concise, powerful tool for anyone ready to lead their organization into a successful future."

—**RAZA SHAIKH,** MANAGING DIRECTOR, LAUNCHPAD VENTURE GROUP, AND COHOST, *ON BOARDS PODCAST*
—**JOE AYOUB,** PRESIDENT, VARUNA STRATEGIES, AND COHOST, *ON BOARDS PODCAST*

"Nothing is riskier than entrepreneurship while also being exciting and potentially rewarding. Rick Williams provides a unique and highly valuable appreciation of what it takes to achieve that success with a consistent commitment to innovation and personal grit and an absolute focus on making the tough decisions in the real world of tight budgets and limited resources. *Create the Future* is a must-read for any leader working through the opportunities and challenges of innovation."

—**JACK DERBY,** FOUNDER, DERBY CENTER OF ENTREPRENEURSHIP AT TUFTS UNIVERSITY; SERIAL ENTREPRENEUR; AND CEO, DERBY MANAGEMENT

"*Create the Future* is a very practical handbook providing a step-by-step guide to understanding crises, understanding oneself, and making better decisions. I fully support the recommended approach of forming a CTF Team with one or two external individuals whom you trust. The CTF leadership Team Exercises are very handy and useful.""

—**YI MA,** FOUNDER, HERITAN CAPITAL; GLOBAL SHAPERS COMMUNITY MEMBER, WORLD ECONOMIC FORUM; AND FORMER INVESTIGATING JOURNALIST, CCTV (CHINA)

"In *Create the Future*, Rick Williams offers a comprehensive guide for leaders seeking to navigate the complexities of decision-making, strategic planning, and implementation—making it a valuable resource for individuals and organizations aiming to be stronger and more confident in shaping success in a largely unknown future."

—**HENRIK TOTTERMAN, D.SC.,** PROFESSOR OF PRACTICE, HULT BOSTON; TEACHING FACULTY, HARVARD; CEO OF LEADX3M LLC; AND HONORARY CONSUL OF FINLAND IN NEW ENGLAND

"For most of us, imagining that we can shape the future is an intimidating challenge. Rick Williams demonstrates that we have a hand in how our future emerges. It is both possible and a requirement of leadership to tackle this challenge. *Create the Future* provides a roadmap on the journey, with leadership team exercises to find the future that works for any organization. With readable and tangible examples, this book gives the reader confidence that Creating the Future is within our reach."

—**TOM DOORLEY,** CHAIR AND FOUNDER, SAGE PARTNERS, LLC; FORMER SENIOR PARTNER, DELOITTE CONSULTING; AND HOST OF THE PODCAST *FOCUS ON THE GROWTH: SAGE INSIGHTS*

"Rick Williams's book *Create the Future* is based on the experiences of successful corporate strategic management consultants and business leaders. As China undergoes a dual transformation in both industrial and economic forms, this book offers successful entrepreneurs in China inspiration from the experiences of successful enterprises in developed countries. *Create the Future* encourages dialogue and the free exchange of ideas as the path to sustained success."

"Rick Williams 的《创造未来》一书基于企业战略管理顾问和商业领袖的成功经验编写。在中国处于产业形态和经济形态双重转型时刻，可以为中国的成功企业家从发达国家成功企业的经验中得到启发。《创造未来》鼓励通过对话和思想的自由交流来实现持续成功。"

—**SHIYU WANG,** SENIOR RESEARCHER AT TAIHE THINK TANK; FOUNDER OF D12 AND DVI

王世渝
太和智库高级研究员
D12及DVI创始人
资深投资银行家

www.amplifypublishinggroup.com

Create the Future: Powerful Decision-Making Tools for Your Company and Yourself

©2024 Rick Williams. No part of this publication may be reproduced, stored in a retrieval system or transmitted in any form by any means electronic, mechanical, or photocopying, recording or otherwise without the permission of the author.

For more information, please contact:
Amplify Publishing, an imprint of Amplify Publishing Group
620 Herndon Parkway, Suite 220
Herndon, VA 20170
info@amplifypublishing.com

Library of Congress Control Number: 2023922679
CPSIA Code: PRV0524A
ISBN-13: 978-1-63755-913-0

Printed in the United States

I dedicate this book to the wonderful and generous people in my life who saw something in an awkward kid who could not spell. My parents, Dick and Betty Williams, kept nudging and helping me deal with my limitations. This book is dedicated to my teachers and professors who saw potential in a student who was good at math and also wrote poetry.

This book is also dedicated to my bosses who mentored me and saw potential beyond what I saw. I have won many sailing regattas as a skipper. I could not have been successful without the teammates who taught me how to be a leader during the good times and the bad times.

CREATE THE FUTURE

**Powerful Decision-Making Tools
for Your Company and Yourself**

RICK WILLIAMS

FOREWORD   1

GETTING STARTED   5
Is this book for you? How to create the future. Chapter summaries.

PART ONE: PREPARE THE COMPANY AND YOURSELF

1. **Create the Future Thinking**   27
   Ask, discover, learn, and decide.
2. **Your Zone of Leadership**   49
   You are not the company. Choose your own future.
3. **The Leader's Role**   67
   Decision Maker, Leader of the Company, and Team Leader.
4. **Engage the Team**   83
   Decision Makers and trusted advisors create the future together.

PART TWO: DEFINE THE CHALLENGE

5. **Define the Challenge**   103
   Solve the right problem.

PART THREE: IMAGINE SUCCESS

6. **Success, Goals, and Values**   111
   What success looks like.

PART FOUR: CREATE OPTIONS

7. **Paths to Success**   127
   Different ways to solve the problem.
8. **Choices for the Future**   137
   Create options for the path to success.

PART FIVE: EVALUATE BARRIERS TO SUCCESS

9. **Execution Barriers** — 149
   Getting there from here.
10. **Key Assumptions** — 171
    What you assume will happen and will not happen.

PART SIX: CHOOSE THE FUTURE

11. **Decision Agenda** — 185
    What decisions must I make?
12. **Prepare to Choose** — 195
    Understand the "meaning" of your decision.
13. **Choose the Future** — 213
    Decide.
14. **Implementation** — 239
    Make it happen.

APPENDIX

Appendix A: *Chapter Key Takeaways* — 247
Appendix B: *Team Exercises and Work Products* — 253

ACKNOWLEDGMENTS — 261
ABOUT THE AUTHOR — 265

FOREWORD

Eight years as the CEO of Vistage Worldwide—one of the world's largest executive coaching organizations for small and mid-sized businesses—has confirmed more than ever my belief that business leaders are catalysts for change, and their ability to foster an environment conducive to innovation and growth is directly proportional to their capacity for open-mindedness. In *Create the Future*, Rick Williams echoes this sentiment, further emphasizing the importance of leaders embracing the feedback of others and leveraging the wealth of experiences they offer as invaluable learning opportunities for other leaders.

Rick masterfully articulates that impactful leadership is rooted in the willingness to not only tolerate but to actively seek diverse perspectives from trusted peers and remain open-minded when facing important decisions. In my own career, I've met with thousands of best-in-class leaders and can say with certainty that a mindset of curiosity plays a key role in a leader's success.

I first discovered the value of diverse perspectives through CEO peer advisory more than two decades ago when I was brand new to the C-suite. Since then, I've seen firsthand how peer advisory groups serve as a sounding board for business leaders spanning a multitude of industries and backgrounds, giving leaders a safe space to come together to troubleshoot issues, share best practices, and receive and offer unbiased feedback with an experienced mentor leading the charge.

Our experience at Vistage demonstrates that world-class leaders who prioritize their connections with other CEOs and business leaders across various industries are more successful leaders of their companies. These peers understand the intricacies and trials of the C-suite while bringing fresh insight unhampered by institutional knowledge. Engaging with leaders from other sectors enables CEOs to openly discuss challenges and gain genuine, objective feedback.

Create the Future encourages leaders to participate in peer support groups like Vistage and to create leadership advisory teams within their organization. Leaders who make these teams into creative engines and encourage and allow different viewpoints to emerge are forming a powerful resource for the success of the company and their success as a leader.

A wide variety of viewpoints fosters creative thinking and mitigates the all-too-common perils of groupthink and confirmation bias. When a CEO solely relies on their own perspective, molded by merely their lived experiences, they can fail to consider important new information. Being surrounded by diverse perspectives from a wide variety of industries and backgrounds makes it easier to identify and challenge preconceived notions. To truly open their minds to these various perspectives, great CEOs listen first and try to be clear about the issue without giving in to the temptation of wanting to correct people or continue to give additional context.

In the continued face of disruption, adopting and maintaining an optimistic mindset remains pivotal. Rick outlines how a positive mindset empowers leaders to concentrate on what is within their control and to take action, rather than make excuses for setbacks.

Through his insightful anecdotes and compelling case studies in *Create the Future*, Rick invites leaders to embrace the boundless opportunities that arise from diverse perspectives. He champions the notion that by fostering an environment where voices are heard, valued, and integrated, leaders can cultivate sustainable growth and enduring impact.

Create the Future is a powerful tool for leaders who are striving to improve their decision-making. When leaders make better decisions, the benefits ripple through their companies, families, and communities.

Sam Reese, CEO
Vistage Worldwide

GETTING STARTED
Is this book for you? How to Create the Future.
Chapter summaries.

I'm a straightforward guy, so I'll start by making clear who this book was *not* written for.

If you are:

- Content with where your organization is today
- Certain you know where the organization will go
- Satisfied with where you are professionally and your career going forward

Please put this book down and walk away.

Create the Future™* is for leaders facing an important opportunity or threat. If you are that leader and want to engage your leadership team's full resources to help you choose the future for your organization, *Create the Future* is the guidebook for making that happen.

Create the Future (CTF) is for leaders who want to imagine where their organization could go, define its best options, and develop a concrete plan for getting there. This book is for leaders of companies, nonprofits, government agencies, and any organization who believe the decisions they make will create the future for their organization and for themselves.

* CREATE THE FUTURE IS A REGISTERED TRADEMARK OWNED BY RICHARD WILLIAMS.

Getting you started is the goal of this chapter.
You will get an overview of the Create the Future process and how you can use it when making important decisions. I will introduce tools you and your leadership team can use to imagine the future and choose the path forward while best expressing your goals, risk preferences, and values.

This chapter's topics are:

Will This Book Make You a More Successful Leader?
The Create the Future process begins by defining the problem and goes step by step to choosing the path forward for your organization. You will creatively identify alternatives and realistically assess your options. Your job is to create the future by the decisions you make. CTF gives you the tools and the structured methodology for doing that.

My Experiences
My direct experience as a management consultant, company founder, team leader, and board member informs my convictions reflected in *Create the Future*. I have drawn from my experience working with a wide range of private and public organizations and leaders with different styles and strengths.

Core Ideas Underlying CTF
The Create the Future process builds on three Convictions about successful leadership and three Leadership Principles.

How to Use This Book to Create the Future
This book can be your GUIDE for improving your skills as a leader. CTF can also be your GUIDEBOOK for planning and decision-making.

A Chapter-by-Chapter Snapshot
The Chapter Snapshot gives you an overview of the book's organization and a sense of how each step of the Create the Future process works.

I USE THE WORD "COMPANY" IN THIS BOOK AS A SHORTHAND FOR YOUR ORGANIZATION, WHETHER IT IS A FOR-PROFIT COMPANY, A NONPROFIT, A GOVERNMENT AGENCY, OR A DEPARTMENT IN A LARGER ORGANIZATION.

WILL THIS BOOK MAKE YOU A MORE SUCCESSFUL LEADER?

Let's begin with who will benefit from the CTF approach to thinking creatively about where your company COULD go and deciding where it WILL go.

Create the Future is a structured methodology for defining the challenge, clarifying success, developing realistic options, evaluating barriers to achieving success, and making decisions without a big consulting-firm price tag.

Every day we quickly make decisions based on our experience, instincts, gut feelings, preconceived ideas, prejudices, preferences, and occasional good judgment. Create the Future is the approach you should use when an important decision with long-term implications is on the line and you must make the best decision possible.

Larger companies have a planning staff and can engage outside strategy and planning support. But leaders of all organizations—from two start-up founders working at a dining room table to the division manager of a multibillion-dollar company—must decide where their organizations will go, whether they have a "planning budget" or not.

Create the Future is a game plan, handbook, and field guide. It offers a detailed, structured process that you and your team can use without hiring a business consultant or team facilitator. CTF begins by defining the Challenge—the opportunity or threat—and guides you through each step until you choose the path forward. So, for example, the CTF process works well for:

- ▸ The CEO who sees a major opportunity to expand the business and wants to engage his leadership team to help decide how to pursue it
- ▸ The start-up founders who are unsure of what path to take to leverage an innovative business concept
- ▸ The owner of a company with declining revenues who wants help discovering how to turn the company around
- ▸ The economic development agency director who wants to be sure

the organization is focused on the big challenges emerging in the next decade
- ▸ The midlevel manager who wants to use top-level planning and organizational-development tools to enhance the department's value in the larger organization
- ▸ The board of directors that wants the CEO and senior managers to take a disciplined approach to developing the company's five-year business plan

I wrote *Create the Future* for organizations large and small. Yes, the decisions facing the CEO of John Hancock Insurance, for example, are different in scale from those facing the YMCA board in Provo, Utah. Yes, implementing decisions will be more complex for an international company than for a regional service organization.

But the elements of a successful decision-making process are the same. *Create the Future* presents a straightforward, concrete method for making practical and implementable decisions. It guides leaders through the fundamental, hands-on process of gathering quantitative and qualitative information, creatively identifying alternatives, and realistically assessing the options. *CTF* then gives leaders the decision-making tools to make decisions expressing their goals, risk preferences, and values.

Some organizations can afford to hire McKinsey, Deloitte, or BCG to prepare consultant reports and take them through the planning and decision-making process. Having worked as a management consultant for many years, I know the value talented and experienced consultants can bring to their clients. If your firm can hire a qualified business consulting firm, do it. Engaging an outside consultant can be a valuable addition to the planning effort. The consultant will gather new information and get outside perspectives difficult for your firm to secure. In some cases, the consultant will compile and analyze information already available in your organization and put it in a format better suited to evaluating the decisions you must make.

But most organizations cannot hire major outside consulting support. CTF shows you how to build an internal Team that will become your

Create the Future is a structured methodology for defining the problem, clarifying success, developing realistic options, evaluating barriers to achieving success, and making decisions without a big consulting-firm price tag.

"consultant." What the CTF Team knows, who the Team knows, and what the Team can learn will be the basis for the decisions you must make. And the Team's insights and recommendations will broaden and enrich your decision-making.

If you hire outside consultants, use the CTF process to guide your internal analysis and decision-making. Integrate the consultant's work into the CTF process, with your Team doing the core evaluation and decision-making.

MY EXPERIENCES

Before I introduce the CTF process and describe what you will learn, I want to share some of my experience that I bring to this book.

My goal in writing *Create the Future* was to put the processes and tools a top-line leadership consulting firm would bring to an engagement in a form you can use on your own or with limited outside support.

The processes and tools offered in *Create the Future* are the product of decades of experience and learning. I founded an award-winning company and was a management consultant. I have served as a board of directors member and board chair. I have worked with major international firms, large national government agencies, technology start-ups, and regional nonprofits.

For part of my career, I was a management consultant with Arthur D. Little, Inc. (ADL), a large global consulting firm. Companies worldwide hired ADL to help solve complex business and technology problems. (For example, two instruments that landed on the moon were built at ADL.) Much of my work was with large organizations that hired us to support strategy evaluations, market and technology analysis, risk assessments, and team building and facilitation. I helped clients understand where the organization could go and decide which path to choose.

I founded and was president of The Equity Company, Inc., a real estate development and investment company that won multiple awards for its residential development projects and for public/private partnerships that developed affordable housing.

I have also studied with scholars of business strategy and finance at Harvard Business School.

I have worked with leaders who were certain of their vision and not open to other points of view. I have worked with leaders whose world was changing around them but would not adapt their organization to the new environment to survive. I have also worked with leaders who set up forums to engage with their staff and learn from their insights.

My direct experience with a wide range of private and public organizations and leaders with different styles and strengths informs my convictions reflected in *Create the Future.* From each experience—and carefully watching how their organizations subsequently fared—I learned the importance of being open to new ideas and perspectives and learning from others.

I have also drawn insight from my nonprofessional passion—sailboat racing. (In fact, I have often thought about writing a book titled *Everything I Know about Leadership I Learned on My Sailboat.*) I have been privileged to lead extraordinary sailing crews. These small groups of unpaid men and women show up on race day for one reason: to be part of a high-performance team striving to win that day's race.

We did not win every race, but over the years, we have won many local and regional sailing championships. My experiences recruiting, training, and leading those high-performance and high-expectations crews inform many of my convictions about leadership. And they contribute to CTF's approach to setting goals and achieving success.

CORE IDEAS UNDERLYING CTF

My experiences have led me to three Convictions about successful leadership. These Convictions underpin the Create the Future process.

I can create the future.

Leaders create the future for their organization—and for themselves—by the choices they make and the decisions they make.

I can learn from others.

Leaders who collaborate with their leadership teams to better understand the opportunity or threat and to identify a range of options for addressing the Challenge will make better decisions—and more successfully execute on those decisions.

My decisions can express my goals, risk preferences, and values.

Few decisions are, in themselves, "right" or "wrong," except as viewed from the future. The leader's challenge is to fully understand the options available and match them to their goals, risk preferences, and values.

Convictions and Principles

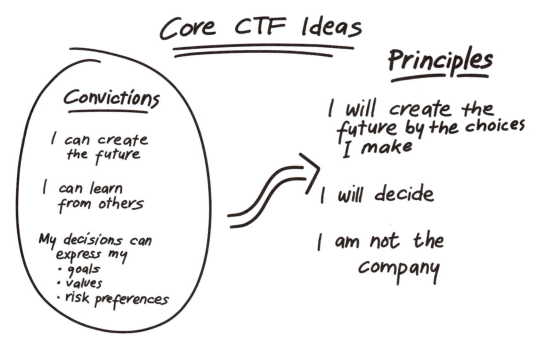

Underlying these three Convictions are three Leadership Principles that guide the Create the Future process:

I will create the future by the choices I make.

I will decide.

I am not the company.

Let me elaborate on each of these Principles.

I Will Create the Future by the Choices I Make

We see Tesla, Amazon, and Google grow and thrive. Others like Sears Roebuck, Blockbuster Video, and Polaroid were successful and then declined as they failed to adapt. The leaders of these companies and organizations of all sizes create the future by the decisions they make.

Creative innovation and the courage to choose—to decide—are essential for success. Not adapting to change and an unwillingness to choose are the paths to failure.

> *One day, Amazon will fail . . . We have to try to delay that day for as long as possible.*
>
> —Jeff Bezos, founder of Amazon,
> at a company-wide meeting in 2018

Jensen Huang built chipmaker Nvidia, which became the core technology underlying artificial intelligence (AI), with the slogan, "Our company is thirty days from going out of business." Huang started making chips for video games and then drove innovation step by step until Nvidia found the AI market and became a trillion-dollar company.

> *If you don't internalize that sensibility, you will go out of business.*
> —Jensen Huang, founder of Nvidia

Believing you can and will create the future is foundational to being an impactful leader.

Leaders like Bezos and Huang built their companies on creative innovation—thinking broadly about the options they had—and on a determination to choose—to make decisions that created their companies' future.

The fundamental starting concept of CTF is that leaders create the future by the choices they make. As the leader of the organization, your responsibility is to develop and communicate a vision of the future, to make decisions on behalf of the organization, and to lead the organization as it executes on its plans. Believing you can and will create the future is foundational to being an impactful leader.

There is a dichotomy in saying, "*I will create the future*" while also knowing that we do not completely control the future and cannot dictate the future of our organization with precision. We do not control many things in our lives. Death and taxes are two of them. That is the nature of life.

As humans, we remember the past and anticipate the future. Leadership is a purposeful connection of what we do today with what will happen tomorrow. We cannot dictate the future, but our decisions today are important determinants of what will happen tomorrow. Your job as the leader is to create and manage a process for moving your organization into the future with purpose.

Professor Dan Gilbert from Harvard's psychology department relates the research on humans' unique ability to think about the future. But he argues that we have difficulty thinking about a future different from the world around us today.

> *We insist on steering our boats because we think we have a pretty good idea of where we should go, but the truth is that much of our steering is in vain . . . the future is fundamentally different than it appears through the prospectiscope (the act of looking forward).*
> —Dan Gilbert, *Stumbling on Happiness*

As an impactful leader, you are creating a vision of the future for your company different from a simple continuation of where it is today. And you are choosing the path forward most likely to realize that vision. Your job is to set the company on a course with an understood prospect of success and to prepare the organization to face the challenges of executing on the choices you make.

> *Leadership is a journey, not a destination.*
> *It is a marathon, not a sprint.*
> *It is a process, not an outcome.*
>
> —John Donahoe, president of eBay,
> as quoted by Bill George in *True North*

I Will Decide

Create the Future is about making decisions. CTF is a structured methodology for clarifying goals, developing realistic options, and making decisions.

The language of "decisions" helps you, as a leader, be clear to yourself and to others that your job is to make decisions. Making decisions is hard. Seldom are there easy choices. Your team and shareholders may have firmly held conflicting views. As you think about your role as a leader, keep your responsibility to decide in clear focus.

Deciding is choosing. Using CTF, you will create future options for the company. You will clarify your goals, your risk preferences, and your values. There is no CTF prescription for which decision is right for you. Create the Future is about how to decide, not what to decide. Choosing the future is your responsibility.

I Am Not the Company

As the leader, you must make decisions on behalf of "the company." You must also recognize that you are not the company. Your duties to the company and to yourself are separate and different. You are responsible for leading the company. You are also responsible for your own life and the welfare of your family.

I outline tools you can use to identify your Zone of Leadership—where your passions and strengths overlap—on a track separate from your work with the CTF Team. Knowing your Zone of Leadership and the professional role best expressing your Zone of Leadership will make you a better leader of your organization.

Create the Future is about how to decide, not what to decide. Choosing the future is your responsibility.

HOW TO USE THIS BOOK TO CREATE THE FUTURE

There are two ways to use this book. *CTF* can be your GUIDE for improving your skills as a leader. *CTF* can be your GUIDEBOOK for planning and decision-making.

Guide for Improving Your Skills

Create the Future's planning and decision-making process is a tutorial for developing your skills as a leader. Mastering each step in the CTF process will strengthen your understanding of leadership skills and thoughtful planning. CTF will also build your understanding of your own skills and passions.

The CTF approach will strengthen your skills and decision-making when addressing major challenges. You will:

- Think more deeply about success and goals
- Create a broader range of choices
- Better understand the barriers and risks of the options you have
- Make better decisions for your organization and for yourself
- Design your professional path as an expression of your skills, passions, and personal goals

Guidebook for Creating the Future

Create the Future is a "How-To Field Guide" for creating the future. *Create the Future*—including the Team exercises—gives you a structured process for starting with a challenge and ending with a decision. *CTF* guides you and your leadership team through each step. The exercises capture information, develop options, and clarify judgments you will make when choosing your organization's path forward.

CTF gives you a methodology with planning and decision-making tools to use when making important decisions. Some of these tools I developed, and others I adapted from those used by leading consultants, coaches, and skilled leaders.

- *Categories of Future Choices*—categories of options for achieving success
- *Key Assumptions*—your assumptions made explicit
- *Why Should We Care?*—why anyone other than you should care about the company's future
- *Barriers to Execution*—the probability of successful execution from where you are today
- *Benefits and Barriers Matrix*—display of benefits and barriers
- *Success, Risk, and Values Profile*—display of qualitative characteristics
- *Your Zone of Leadership*—the overlap of your Strengths and Passions

"I don't have time for the Team exercises!" If you "just don't have time" to put a CTF Team together and have two or three meetings to help you work through the issues, use the CTF process steps even when the Team is just you and you must decide tomorrow.

CTF is a tool kit. Understand the CTF concepts, and then select the elements most helpful to you. Brainstorming—"all ideas are good ideas"—will help you imagine what you could do. The decision-making tools will help your board, executive committee, or family members make better decisions supported, or accepted, by most members.

You will not have time to do each CTF exercise beginning with defining the challenge and ending with choosing the future. Select the most impactful exercises for your situation. And use the other exercises as a checklist to be sure you have considered and understand the issues these exercises raise.

A Quick Introduction to How CTF Works

Prepare Your Company and Yourself

I recommend that you ask at least two trusted advisors to work with you as you plan the future for your organization. These advisors, plus you, will be the CTF Team. You may have an executive committee or a board of directors. They can be the Team, and you can add one or two others.

Before starting the Team's work, invest preparation time getting clear about your goals for the Team's work. You may also benefit from looking at your personal and professional goals as context for the Team's work by finding your Zone of Leadership.

Preparation is the topic of this book's first chapters.

> CREATE THE FUTURE THINKING
> YOUR ZONE OF LEADERSHIP
> THE LEADER'S ROLE
> ENGAGE THE TEAM

Five Steps to Creating the Future

Building on the core leadership principles, *Create the Future* guides you through a deceptively simple five-step process.

> **STEP 1.** DEFINE THE CHALLENGE
> **STEP 2.** IMAGINE SUCCESS
> **STEP 3.** CREATE OPTIONS
> **STEP 4.** EVALUATE BARRIERS
> **STEP 5.** CHOOSE THE FUTURE

Why do I say the process is "deceptively" simple? Because performing each of the five steps pulls on the complex network of strings connected to your company's organization, finances, leadership, culture, market position, technology, and ownership.

The Create the Future process encourages you to define what success would look like and to articulate your values and risk preferences. CTF guides you, your leadership team, and your key advisors as you define the organization's goals. CTF brings to the table the best information, options, and assessments available.

Create the Future, Five Steps

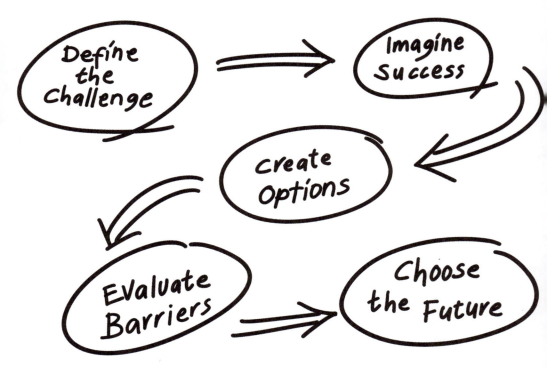

And CTF gives you a more comprehensive understanding of your options, including the risks and values attached to each. The information will not be perfect. Understanding where there is uncertainty and specifying the assumptions you are making are part of the process. CTF brings you to the point where you can decide—where you must decide.

Create the Future's five steps are not, in themselves, original to this book. The CTF tools are similar to those a top-line consultant and coach would use. What is wholly original is *Create the Future*'s total package of concepts, processes, and exercises presented in a format that enables you to go from defining the challenge to making a decision. The totality of this concrete package—integrating process and tools—is *Create the Future*'s unique contribution.

Create the Future Thinking

Underlying the CTF process is a specific approach to problem-solving and decision-making—an attitude called Create the Future Thinking. Create the Future Thinking is an "ask-questions, discover-what-you-know, and learn-from-what-you-discover" approach to making important decisions. You strengthen your decision-making by using these four steps each time you take your Team through a problem-solving process or work through a challenge on your own.

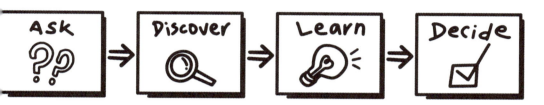

The Create the Future Thinking four-step approach improves your success prospects by empowering you to understand what you know, learn from what you know (and what you don't know), and focus on what you must decide.

Capture What You Create—The Decision Book and the Decision Package

Capturing the information and insights created by the Team exercises in a form directly usable by you and other Decision Makers is central to CTF's success. A Decision Book is the CTF Team's "report to the Decision Makers." The Decision Book is a loose-leaf, three-ring binder or Google Docs folder with Team Meeting Notes and exercise work products. It includes the decisions to be made, the choices available, and the Team's analysis of the choices.

Before the Decision Makers' meeting to choose the path forward for the organization, the CTF Team Leader will draw material from the Decision Book and prepare a Decision Package. It becomes part of the Decider's meeting agenda for making the final decisions and includes the decisions to be made and a summary of the Future Choices under consideration.

Team Exercises—A Facilitated Team Format

The Team exercises are written in a facilitated format assuming a facilitator or meeting leader is at the whiteboard asking questions of participating Team members. In Chapter 4, "Engage the Team," I recommend that you, as the company leader, get someone else to lead or facilitate the Team exercises. You will get more from the exercises as a contributor and as a witness to the discussion. You will have more time to absorb and consider what you are hearing.

If you are doing the exercises with one or two others, you will not have a "facilitator." Designate one of you to be the notetaker. If you are doing the exercises by yourself, answer the questions and write down your keyword answers. Recording your ideas in writing is the best way to build a record of your thinking, which becomes the basis for your learning and for developing your thinking.

Adapt the exercise format and the questions to your circumstances and to your issues.

A CHAPTER-BY-CHAPTER SNAPSHOT

The following is an overview of this book's organization and the contributions of each chapter. The chapter summaries profile each Create the Future step and connect the steps into a coherent process for making difficult decisions.

PART ONE: PREPARE THE COMPANY AND YOURSELF

Chapter 1. Create the Future Thinking

Before getting into the step-by-step CTF approach, this chapter introduces the process tools underlying CTF. I describe elements of Create the Future Thinking along with techniques you can use to make your Team into a creative engine for the organization.

Chapter 2. Your Zone of Leadership

You are not the company. Clarity about your strengths, passions, and professional goals will make you a better leader of your organization. This chapter gives you the tools to find your Zone of Leadership—leadership roles expressing both your passions and your strengths.

Chapter 3. The Leader's Role

You are the leader of the organization or the company's owner. Before engaging others, such as the CTF Team, to look at the challenges facing the company, profile your understanding of the challenge and what success would look like to you. Create a statement explaining why others should care about how the company responds to the challenge.

Chapter 4. Engage the Team

In most situations, you will benefit more from the CTF process if you organize a "CTF Team" to go through the exercises with you and other Decision Makers. The Team could be a board of directors, company founders or owners, or an executive committee. You can add key staff and outside advisors to the Team. This chapter describes who should be on the Team, its role, and the work it will do.

PART TWO: DEFINE THE CHALLENGE

Chapter 5. Define the Challenge

Begin by solving the right problem. Too frequently, we respond to the symptoms and not the underlying problem. Begin the CTF work by being sure you understand the opportunity, threat, or issue you are addressing.

PART THREE: IMAGINE SUCCESS

Chapter 6. Success, Goals, and Values

Having identified the opportunity, threat, or issue facing the company, work through what a successful response would look like, including the values it would express. Specify the operational goals that will define when success has been achieved.

PART FOUR: CREATE OPTIONS

Chapter 7. Paths to Success

Before jumping to a quick conclusion about what is the best response to the challenge facing the organization, broaden your thinking. Imagine different Categories of Future Choices—ways success could be achieved—before imagining specific initiatives for reaching the organization's goals.

Chapter 8. Choices for the Future

Using the Categories of Future Choices as the framework, imagine initiatives the organization could undertake to achieve success. "All ideas are good ideas" is the creative start of this work. Then, with many ideas in hand, narrow the possible options to a handful of Choices for the Future to be considered in detail.

PART FIVE: EVALUATE BARRIERS TO SUCCESS

Chapter 9. Execution Barriers

The most creative initiatives with big potential will not realize their value if you cannot implement them successfully. Understanding the execution risks of each Future Choice is the work of this chapter. The execution risk analysis will inform your assessment of the options when choosing which Future Choice to pursue.

Chapter 10. Key Assumptions

Underlying virtually every decision we make are assumptions about what will or will not happen. You will better understand the risk profile of the options you are considering and the decisions you will make when you are clear about the assumptions you are making. CTF encourages Decision Makers to share the assumptions they are making.

PART SIX: CHOOSE THE FUTURE

Chapter 11. Decision Agenda

Whether to launch a new product may be a simple Yes-or-No decision. More often, a series or network of decisions will be required. In this chapter, you outline the Decision Tree of critical decisions and define the decisions you must make.

Chapter 12. Prepare to Choose

The Team, including the Decision Makers, do a final check on whether they are ready to choose the company's future. They answer the question, "What is the meaning of each option we have?" The Deciders can ask for the Team's recommendations for the decisions to be made.

Chapter 13. Choose the Future

The Team has done its work, and the Decision Makers' work begins. Each Decider identifies the assumptions they are making and has an opportunity to learn from other Deciders as they talk through their perspectives and reasons for preferring one Choice over another. Finally, the Decision Makers will choose the path forward.

Chapter 14. Implementation

Great ideas have little value without successful execution. This chapter briefly outlines the implementation next steps: create a vision, develop an execution plan, and manage the execution plan.

APPENDIX

Appendix A—Key Takeaways of each chapter
Appendix B—Team Exercises and their Work Products

LET'S GET STARTED

I know your job as leader is difficult. You are expected to set a direction for the organization when the options and their possible outcomes are uncertain.

You are also an individual with your own strengths and weaknesses and your own hopes and fears.

I wrote *Create the Future* to give you the tools to make the best decisions possible. You will choose the future by the decisions you make. And your job is to make those decisions.

Now that you know how the Create the Future process works, let's put it into action!

> **KEY TAKEAWAYS**
>
> At the end of each chapter, you will see a short list of Key Takeaways. These are core ideas and concepts I want you to take away from that chapter.
>
> Here are the Key Takeaways from this chapter.
>
> 1. The Create the Future process is a structured methodology for defining the problem, clarifying success, developing realistic options, evaluating barriers to achieving success, and making decisions without a big consulting-firm price tag.
> 2. Believing you can and will create the future is foundational to being an impactful leader.
> 3. Create the Future is about how to decide, not what to decide. Choosing the future is your responsibility.
> 4. You are not the company. Your duties to the company and to yourself are separate and different.

PART 1: PREPARE THE COMPANY AND YOURSELF

▼

PART 2: DEFINE THE CHALLENGE

▼

PART 3: IMAGINE SUCCESS

▼

PART 4: CREATE OPTIONS

▼

PART 5: EVALUATE BARRIERS TO SUCCESS

▼

PART 6: CHOOSE THE FUTURE

Chapter Topics

IDG Becomes an All-Digital Platform Company

Create the Future Thinking

Creativity—The Power of Your Team

Measuring Longitude—The Right Idea from the Wrong Person

CHAPTER 1

CREATE THE FUTURE THINKING
Ask, discover, learn, and decide.

Create the Future is a structured methodology for defining the problem, clarifying goals, developing realistic options, and making decisions without paying a big consulting fee. Create the Future Thinking is an attitude, a way of approaching difficult situations.

This chapter outlines Create the Future Thinking and describes tools you will use to think creatively about where you are today and where you could go tomorrow. These techniques will turn you and your team into a creative powerhouse, and you will better understand the issues you are facing and the meaning of your decisions.

This chapter also includes two stories. One is about how the CEO of IDG used the tools core to Create the Future Thinking to transform the company's business model during COVID-19. The second story is about national leaders who would not accept the solution to a major problem facing them from someone who was not of their professional ranks.

This chapter's topics are:

IDG Becomes an All-Digital Platform Company
IDG's new CEO transformed the world's leading technology research and events company into a digital platform company using tools similar to CTF Thinking.

Create the Future Thinking
Create the Future Thinking is the ask, discover, learn, and decide approach to better understanding the issues and the options before making decisions.

Creativity—The Power of Your Team
With encouragement and your permission, your team will become a creative engine for discovering the best path forward.

Measuring Longitude—The Right Idea from the Wrong Person
Measuring where ships are at sea East and West was essential to British commerce and naval power. Solving the problem was so difficult that Parliament offered a large cash prize. But a royal committee would not give the prize to John Harrison because he was not of their professional class and his method for measuring longitude was different than the astronomical solution they anticipated.

Before deciding how you will respond to a difficult challenge, pause and be sure you understand the problem and the available options. Even when you are working through a difficult issue by yourself, you will make better decisions if you follow the CTF five-step process. However, I encourage you to engage with others using the CTF creative tools to explore and expand your thinking.

> *It does not make sense to hire smart people and then tell them what to do. We hire smart people so they can tell us what to do.*
> —Steve Jobs, founder and CEO of Apple,
> *Steve Jobs: His Own Words and Wisdom*

CTF Conviction: I can learn from others.
When I face a difficult decision, I want to know if there are other ways to think about the problem—to be sure I understand the problem and not simply its symptoms. Yes, I must choose in the end. But my decision is more likely to be successful when I am open to engaging with others and hearing other points of view. Using the CTF approach, I will also build a shared understanding of and commitment to solving the problem within my leadership team.

In this chapter I share two leadership stories. The first is about Mohamad Ali's recovery process after becoming CEO of IDG in the middle of the COVID-19 pandemic. He used techniques similar to the CTF process to transform IDG into a dynamic, global digital platform company. He used team whiteboard exercises to learn, communicate, create, and build commitment.

The second story is about leaders facing a global problem who were not open to hearing the solution to their problem from someone who was not an "expert." I am a sailor, and this is a sailor's story. At a time when ship captains did not have GPS navigation technology and did not know where they were, East and West, while at sea, the British Parliament offered a large cash reward for devising a way to measure a ship's location at sea. The story is about British leaders who were unwilling to accept the solution when it did not come from the kind of person they believed should solve the problem—their professional peers.

IDG BECOMES AN ALL-DIGITAL PLATFORM COMPANY

Mohamad Ali became CEO of IDG in August of 2019—five months before the COVID-19 pandemic. IDG is the world's leading technology media, events, and research company. IDG's technology research reports from its IDC division are the gold standard. Its technology media such as *CIO* magazine are world-renowned, and its events serve as the top convener of technology leaders. If you are bringing new technology to the world market, you likely developed it with IDC's insights, had it written about in an IDG publication, or introduced it to customers at an IDG event.

IDG is well known for its research reports, media, and in-person meetings and conferences for the technology market. When Mohamad became CEO of IDG, he had a well-defined thesis for how IDG could create more value in the marketplace. Mohamad believed that IDG could create an all-digital platform to inform and connect technology sellers and buyers. IDG had the components for an all-digital platform but had not made the connections. He knew from his previous business strategy work that a great strategy has value only if the company can execute on it.

Being new to the company, Mohamad did not know the staff and its culture well. He began his tenure as CEO of IDG by convening whiteboard meetings with his senior staff and the broader employee community. His goals for the meetings were:

▸ Establish himself as the leader of the company

- Build trusting relationships
- Earn acceptance
- Learn from the staff
- Test his ideas

From the team meetings, Mohamad learned that the IDG staff saw themselves as a mature and stable organization performing from a well-established playbook. They did not see themselves as being in the digital platform business or ready to execute a high-growth plan—that was not who they were.

With a better understanding of IDG leadership and culture, Mohamad used the whiteboard team exercises as a vehicle for his leadership team and the staff to:

- Understand the opportunity
- Develop options for exploiting the opportunity
- Create a strategy that IDG could successfully execute
- Communicate the strategic plan and its implementation
- Gain acceptance of the new plans
- Develop within IDG a culture of openness, honesty, and authenticity
- Discover that they could be a high-growth company

The worldwide COVID-19 pandemic shut down IDG's in-person conferences. As Mohamad and his leadership team were exploring the path forward for the company, core components of their business disappeared overnight. Like other organizations dependent on in-person meetings, COVID-19 forced IDG to learn quickly how to do virtual events. IDG became a digital events company on a hurry-up schedule, delivering one thousand virtual events in 2020.

IDG transformed its IDC business's billion-point market model for the $5 trillion technology industry from a static to a dynamic digital platform that allowed technology vendors to have real-time access, including deep analytics. And the media business became a unified global digital platform combining data and human judgment for IDG's two hundred million technology readers.

IDG transformed itself into a fabulously successful digital platform company. The whiteboard-team-meeting approach enabled the IDG staff and the leadership team to develop a plan they understood and accepted. The process moved IDG's staff toward believing they could be a growth company. And IDG became a high-growth company.

Mohamad Ali described the whiteboard meetings and the team's follow-up process as:

- Define the problem.
- Create options.
- Start small and build on the core of understanding and agreement.
- Learn from what works and does not work.
- Take another step.

Mohamad acknowledges that the COVID-19 demands forced changes that otherwise would have been more difficult and taken longer. But the changes would not have happened without a shared acceptance of the plans and goals established by the team whiteboard exercises. (Story taken from a talk given by Mohamad Ali at a Neptune Advisors forum, January 22, 2021.)

CREATE THE FUTURE THINKING

Create the Future Thinking is a discovery and learning process. The four CTF Thinking decision-making steps are:

- Ask
- Discover
- Learn
- Decide

Create the Future Thinking is an ask-questions, discover-what-you-know, and learn-from-what-you-discover process for making important decisions. These four steps are used in each Team exercise presented in this book and should be your mantra when making any difficult decision.

Create the Future Thinking is an ask-questions, discover-what-you-know, and learn-from-what-you-discover process for making important decisions.

CTF Thinking says step back from being certain you know the right thing to do—or from being fearful you do not know what to do. Step back and ask a question. Then think about what you just heard. What did you learn? Now think about what you must decide at this moment, if anything. Pausing to ask, discover, and learn before you decide gives you power. You will also be more centered and in control.

Create the Future Thinking

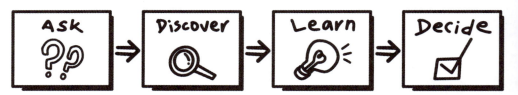

Take a moment to understand the power each step gives you.

Ask Questions

The key to Create the Future Thinking is asking questions. CTF exercises ask the Team questions and record their answers—a seemingly simple approach. Solving the problem begins with asking questions. Simply asking, "Why?" is a powerful place to start.

> *When you are a leader, your job is to have all the questions. You have to be incredibly comfortable looking like the dumbest person in the room. Every conversation you have about a decision, a proposal, or a piece of market information has to be filled with you saying, "What if?" and "Why not?" and "How come?"*
>
> —Jack Welch, former General Electric CEO, *Winning*

I was having dinner with friends on a Friday night when I received a call from the fire department. I owned a multifamily building completing construction. The building was on fire. The fire was mostly out when I arrived, but I was shocked by what I saw. Police car and fire truck lights flashed in the night. Fortunately, no one was living in the building, and there were no injuries.

A fire department inspector asked if he could ask me a few questions as we stood behind a fire truck in the dark. "Of course," was my answer. The "few questions" were forty questions on an interview form about the ownership and history of the building and took thirty minutes to complete. The last question was, "Did you start the fire?" The inspector had a strategy—a Question Strategy—in the structure and sequence of the questions.

Outlining a Question Strategy is a good place to start a Team exercise. A Question Strategy can have elements such as:

▸ Big Picture—What problem are we trying to solve?
▸ Categories of Solutions—Are there categories of possible solutions?
▸ Options—What are possible solutions within the Categories of Solutions?
▸ Research—What do we need to know?

Design a Question Strategy before asking the first question. Your team will answer the question you ask. Your job is to ask the right question. Do you need to understand the problem better? Do you need to imagine different ways you could reach your goals before looking for the best way to get there?

Your job is to ask the right question.

Question Strategy

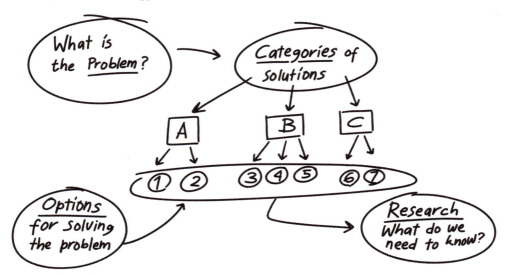

Asking the Team questions captures each Team member's different insights and perspectives. Questioning is the path to discovery and learning. Your understanding of the issues, the choices, and the decisions you must make will change as you listen to other points of view. Stay focused on the decisions you must make rather than the symptoms of the problem before you. In the end, you must choose, but you, as a Decider, will make better decisions after hearing and considering different points of view and different solutions to the problem.

My approach to a new consulting project is to begin the project by writing a detailed outline of the final report, including possible conclusions and recommendations. Yes, the conclusions and recommendations may change as the research progresses. I start with a Question Strategy and an initial assessment of the underlying problem. Drafting possible conclusions and implications of the research forces us to ask, "What will we have to learn, and what information do we need to know to draw these conclusions or different conclusions?" This approach encourages gathering information that's relevant to the decisions to be made rather than to the symptoms that initiated the project.

Questioning is the path to discovery and learning.

Discovering what you know and what you do not know is fundamental to smart decision-making.

What Have We Discovered?

From information brought to the Team meeting and posts on the whiteboard, ask, "What have we discovered?"

- What do we know?
- What can we estimate?
- What don't we know?

Incomplete and uncertain information underlies every decision we make. Your challenge is to understand the quality of the available information and how that quality will shape your decisions. Do you know enough to proceed? Is there inquiry or research you should do?

Decision Makers make better decisions when they:

- Know what they know and do not know
- Understand the quality of the available information
- Identify the assumptions they are making based on the information available

Discovery is learning what you know and do not know. Discovery is also learning what you are assuming will happen or will not happen. The decisions you make will be more soundly founded when you identify what you know, characterize the quality of the available information, and are explicit about your assumptions. Discovering what you know and what you do not know is fundamental to smart decision-making.

We routinely make assumptions about what will happen and what will not happen. Making assumptions in the face of uncertainty is necessary, even required. In the CTF process, the Decision Maker identifies critical assumptions underlying his decisions and communicates the assumptions he is making to himself and to other Deciders.

What Have We Learned?

While *what have we discovered* identifies and characterizes the available information, *what have we learned* is the process of drawing insights from what we discovered. Based on the available information and its level of uncertainty, what inferences can we draw about the challenges we face and our options for going forward?

CTF exercises generate ideas on the whiteboard ranging from completely impractical to profoundly insightful. Once these ideas are on the board, what do you do with them? Learning is making connections, seeing patterns and trends, and realizing what is missing or unknown. Start by asking what these postings tell you about what you know and do not know for:

- The problem you must solve
- Your goals
- Your options
- The decisions you must make

Take all the whiteboard posts and ask:

- Are there connections, patterns, or themes in this data and these ideas?
- Are there different ways of looking at your situation?
- What are the categories of options for addressing the opportunity or threat you face?
- Did you identify a significant new opportunity or obstacle that you need to know more about before going further?
- Are there people or resources you should bring into the conversation?
- Have you identified out-of-bounds areas that were not visible before?
- Is there an experiment you should run or research you should do before going forward?

Learning may not happen until you connect seemingly random data and ideas into a powerful new insight. The recurring question in the Team exercises is "What are we learning?"

Ask Questions and Look for Themes and Patterns

The CTF Team at a Los Angeles–based company making wire used in space satellites is trying to find market opportunities for their highly specialized products. The wire can be coated with copper or even gold and have different diameters for different applications.

Mark is CEO of the company and has asked the Team to suggest products the company could make for companies outside the aerospace industry. Ideas are going on the whiteboard, but no important new opportunities have emerged. The challenge is finding applications where the specialized wiring will add value.

A Team member asks what problem the company's wiring solves for its customers: zero failure, custom-designed for each application, small volume, strength, low maintenance, and corrosion resistance go on the whiteboard.

The discussion then moves to what products or markets value those attributes: robotics, nuclear power plants, and medical devices go on the whiteboard as possible market categories. The Team asks questions and looks for patterns in the suggestions on the board and extrapolates to opportunities that had not surfaced by thinking only about product applications similar to the company's current space applications.

Another challenge question is, "What do we not know that we don't know?" The phrase "you don't know what you don't know" can be said as a throwaway comment, an almost silly thing to say. But asking the Team "what don't we know that we don't know" can lead to an examination of the underlying assumptions in a product or business. What-don't-we-know-that-we-don't-know questions could be formulated as:

- Is there a company outside our business sector that may come into our market?
- Is there a new technology that will make our products obsolete?

▸ Is there a possible future use for technology we control that might be a disruptive product in a different market segment?

Continuously ask, "What don't we know that will change our future?"

Decide

If you are a scholar, your job is to discover and learn. If you are the leader of your organization, your job is to decide—to make decisions for the organization. *Create the Future* is about making better decisions. Use the ask, discover, and learn tools of a scholar, and then decide.

As the leader, your job is to create a vision for the future and make decisions that will take your organization toward that future. CTF encourages you to be clear to yourself and others that you are open to discovery and learning. But also be clear that you will choose—you will decide.

Your Thinking and Discovery Process

Knowing yourself makes you stronger and more resilient. I learn about my thinking by listening to how I explain it to others. *Docendo discimus*—"the best way to learn is to teach." To advance my thinking, I will describe my thinking to a colleague. I make quick first-impression notes and go back to them to clarify my thinking.

And I learn from the experiences of others in similar situations. Rather than asking someone what I should be doing, I ask what they have done when faced with a similar challenge. Most of us do not learn by having someone tell us what to do.

What worked for my colleague may be different from what will work for me in a similar circumstance. But I can learn from her experience. Understanding and strengthening your thinking and discovery process will make you more confident and effective when working through new, complex problems.

Ask, "What don't we know that will change our future?"

CREATIVITY—THE POWER OF YOUR TEAM

Most CTF Team exercises ask for "ideas" and "insights." Getting beyond "just the facts" is the goal. This section profiles techniques you can use to make yourself and your CTF Team into a creative engine for your organization. It will examine the "creative" way of thinking and the importance of giving permission to be open and candid. It will also profile the job of the Team Leader or facilitator and finish with the story about leaders who refused to accept the discovery of a way to measure longitude because the person making the discovery was not from their professional and social circle.

All Ideas Are Good Ideas

For creative work in CTF, the goal is to post lots of ideas on the whiteboard. "There are no bad ideas" is the rule. All ideas are good ideas. Do not ask Team members to propose the "best solution to the problem." Posting only great ideas is not the goal. Ask them to post possible solutions. Team members are responsible for helping find the best solution among those posted. They are not responsible for offering only the best solution and posting it on the whiteboard.

Start where you are today, and set a goal for this creative work, such as the following:

- We have a blockbuster opportunity. Let's take a no-holds-barred look at the best way to exploit this situation.

OR

- This company is doing great. Let's not screw anything up. What are the threats we need to worry about? Are there defensive steps we should take?

Whatever your circumstances, whatever your organization, take down the barriers to thinking about where the organization could go. Develop a Question Strategy beginning with categories of possible solutions to broaden the Team's thinking about options. Imagine many possible approaches and

For creative work, posting lots of ideas on the whiteboard is the goal. Posting only great ideas is not the goal.

---

different ways to think about the issues. A "crazy idea" may suggest a line of thinking that leads to a great idea.

Write on the whiteboard "*All Ideas Are Good Ideas*" and let the magic begin. Use prompts like these to start the idea generation or keep it going:

- What small-change, low risk options can we try?
- What big-change, high-risk options can we imagine?
- We could try . . .
- Another company introduced . . .
- I don't know if we could make this work, but here is an idea.
- Mary's suggestion makes me think of . . .
- You guys are chasing one rabbit. What about this idea?
- If we put these three things together, we would be doing . . .
- If we changed this one thing, we could . . .
- I might be able to get us to . . .
- Keep asking, "What are we learning? What do these ideas suggest?"
- From many possibilities, find connections, themes, insights, and "aha's!"
- Refine many ideas to a few great ideas capable of achieving the goals.

All Ideas Are Good Ideas

We are accustomed to playing our part and being in our place in the culture of our group or organization. Getting into an "all ideas are good ideas" frame of mind is difficult. Find ways to say, "This is not just another meeting." Some groups will have everyone wear something silly to break down our natural inhibitions. Try approaches like this and make it fun!

The Lost Good Idea

When I was a student at Harvard Business School, we worked on a case study about a company selling hand calculators. The professor asked what product the company was selling when marketing a calculator and what product attributes are valuable to potential customers.

I raised my hand and said I wanted the calculator to talk back to me—saying, "I heard you." The professor did not put this attribute idea on the board. Not good for my grade! The professor clearly had "the right answers" in mind, and my customer expectation that a hand calculator would talk back to me was not one of them.

After the class, one of my classmates who had worked at NASA told me the space agency extensively surveyed astronauts on attributes they want in keypad instruments like calculators. One of the primary attributes was "I heard you" feedback. When the astronaut presses a key, she wants to know that the keystroke is entered by a click or another touch sensation.

The professor lost the "I heard you" feature because it did not fit his preconceived idea of a correct answer.

To help get the CTF Team into a creative way of thinking, use ideation techniques for "brainstorming" to generate new ideas. The ideation technique examines the goal or problem elements and imagines different ways to understand each element. Understanding the elements can lead to new ideas for addressing the overall problem.

An example is using the Team Leader question, ". . . the goal we have established for the company is to grow annual revenue each year . . ."

To get the Team's thinking started, ask Who is the company? What products or departments of the company can create new revenues? Ask what "grow" means. Do we want one-time sales, recurring sales, service sales, product sales, and so on? Ask what "grow annual revenue each year" could mean. Are we trying to get revenues to a new, higher level, or are we creating a growth engine to keep growing into the future?

Before asking for ways the company could grow revenues, develop a Question Strategy. Identify different categories of options for growing revenues. The categories of possible growth options are column headings on the whiteboard (see the How to Grow Revenues? illustration that follows).

Then ask for possible ways to grow revenue in each revenue growth category. If the Team was simply asked for revenue growth ideas without first thinking about different ways revenues could be raised (Categories of Future Choices), the suggested initiatives would be fewer and within a narrower band of possibilities.

Question Strategy for How to Grow Revenues

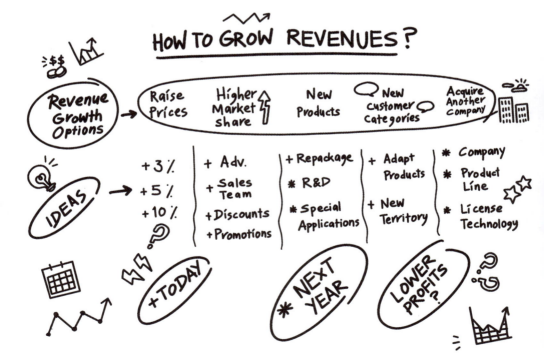

Permission for Candor

Lowering barriers within the CTF Team will encourage more open dialogue. Company owners, the CEO, and members of the board of directors may be part of the Team. Open and frank contributions from everyone are the objective. As a leader and Decision Maker, you must give "permission" for candor by:

- Checking your job title at the door
- Being clear that what is said in the room stays in the room
- Acknowledging all suggestions with respect

As General James Mattis, former U.S. Secretary of Defense, once said, "You know when you make general or admiral in the military, they say, 'Congratulations, General. You will never eat poor food again. And you will never hear the truth again.'"

Harvard Business School professor Amy Edmondson coined the term "psychological safety" to describe a work environment where people feel safe to take risks—where failure is accepted as part of the path to success.

> *Psychological safety helps people take the interpersonal risks that are necessary for achieving excellence in a fast-changing, interdependent world. . . . They know their questions are appreciated, ideas are welcome, and errors and failures are discussable.*
> —Amy Edmondson, *Right Kind of Wrong*

To get the most value from your CTF Team or any core advisors, you must be clear that they have permission to be open and candid and that all contributions are welcome and will be respected. The Team will not discuss some topics without specific permission from the company and Team leadership. The option of selling the company could be an example. Leadership performance expectations are another. Team members will be guided by what senior leaders say and do to establish norms within the Team and set boundaries on Team discussions. The fewer boundaries, the better. Give permission by being clear that all ideas are welcome. Post them on the whiteboard.

Encourage and Discourage

The Team Leader or facilitator must both encourage and discourage. Encourage participation and draw each Team member into the creation process by asking for their suggestions. For example, "Josie, you successfully grew market share with our new product several years ago. What do you think we can do now to grow revenues?" Discourage "that will never work" and "that is a nutty idea" comments at this point.

Also, encourage the Team members to develop their ideas. With an idea posted, ask the person offering it to go further with their thinking and develop the concept into a more fully formed option. As the person offering the idea develops their thinking, those listening will imagine other ideas using a similar line of reasoning. Start the creative virtuous circle.

Hire an Expert Consultant

You might hire outside consulting support to bring "new ideas" into the discussion of where to go or how to solve the problem. Consider engaging academics, industry specialists, and creative consultants. If you have the budget to bring in outside expertise or creative support, do that. Have them prepare a report that becomes input to the Team's work. While hiring an expert to participate as a Team member is an option, I am cautious about having an "expert" participate in a meeting to create new ideas unless it is to present research done for the meeting. I have found that introducing "an expert" into a team meeting often shuts down new thinking by other team members who feel "I am not the expert and don't want to say something and look stupid."

MEASURING LONGITUDE
—THE RIGHT IDEA FROM THE WRONG PERSON

Solving the longitude problem is a historically important and fascinating sailing story. Before telling you the story of how John Harrison—the mechanical tinkerer—solved the longitude problem that Sir Isaac Newton could not solve, I want to share my experience of getting the best idea from someone with the least relevant experience.

I purchased a new sailboat some years ago. Naming your new boat is one of the rituals of boat ownership. I asked sailing and non-sailing friends to come to a boat-naming party to help me find the right name for my boat. I suggested criteria for the name reflecting the experiences I hoped to have on the new boat. During the party, people wrote suggestions for the new boat name on a flip chart I had posted on the wall.

My friends included both very experienced sailors and others who knew nothing about sailing. Many of the suggestions were funny references to the skipper's alleged attributes or missing attributes. A friend who is a professional graphic designer came to the party with a drawing of the name "Ricochet" bouncing off the waterline of the boat.

I was thinking of new adventures and sailing off to distant lands, and I wanted a name that captured my aspirations. During the party, I talked to a woman who was not a sailor. After listening to my story, she suggested naming the boat Voyager, inspired by the name of the Voyager spacecraft launched to explore the outer reaches of our solar system.

I knew that was the right name for my boat the moment I heard the suggestion. Voyager, the boat, won countless regattas and became my brand name within the sailing community of New England. The idea for the name came from someone who was not an expert or even a sailor. Fortunately, I was open to listening to a non-expert's ideas.

In the book *Longitude: The True Story of a Lone Genius Who Solved the Greatest Scientific Problem of His Time*, author Dava Sobel tells a similar story about leaders challenged by a critical problem who would not accept the solution to their problem coming from someone who was not a professional peer or an expert with the correct credentials.

Before 1740 there was no accurate way to measure longitude while at sea. Longitude is the east and west scale measuring your location on the globe. Many ships were lost because they did not know they were sailing onto a rocky coast. When Columbus sailed west from the Canary Islands in 1492, he could not measure how far west he had gone except by counting the number of days sailed and the boat's approximate speed. He sailed west until he hit land.

Great Britain was a maritime power, and accurately navigating the globe was critical for its commercial and naval ships. Reliably measuring longitude was so important that the British Parliament passed the Longitude Act of 1714. They offered a prize for a "practical and useful" way to measure longitude, equivalent to millions of 2024 U.S. dollars. Sir Isaac Newton worked on the problem. The Act established a Longitude Board to evaluate proposals and award prizes. The French and Dutch offered rewards. Finding a solution was believed to be so unlikely that solving the longitude problem became synonymous with inventing a perpetual motion machine.

John Harrison was a carpenter by trade who took an interest in clocks. Harrison built a clock that could be taken to sea and keep accurate time. He showed that a navigator could accurately calculate longitude using his clock. The Harrison clock was set to Greenwich, United Kingdom, time. If a ship is at sea and knows Greenwich time at noon (sun at peak altitude), the navigator will know the number of minutes difference between Greenwich time and the ship's time. The navigator multiplies the speed of the earth's rotation by the number of minutes. The result is the distance east or west of Greenwich and the longitude at the ship's location. Harrison's clock solved the longitude problem.

The British Royal Astronomer was an advisor to the Longitude Board. He believed an astronomer could measure longitude by an astronomical observation such as the rotation of the moons around Jupiter. In his view, the correct answer to the longitude problem was an as-yet-undiscovered astronomical observation. The Royal Astronomer would not agree to give Harrison, the mechanical tinkerer, the longitude prize. After forty years of refusing to acknowledge a solution different from an astronomical observation, King George III and the Parliament convinced the Board to give Harrison a portion of the prize money.

Finding the answer to a complex problem starts with removing boundaries and walking away from preconceived ideas about the "right answer" and who will have the right answer.

KEY TAKEAWAYS
1. Create the Future Thinking is an ask-questions, discover-what-you-know, and learn-from-what-you-discover process for making important decisions.
2. Your job is to ask the right questions.
3. Questioning is the path to discovery and learning.
4. All ideas are good ideas.
5. Discovering what you know and what you do not know is fundamental to smart decision-making.
6. Keep asking, "What are we learning?"
7. Ask, "What don't we know that will change our future?"

PART 1: PREPARE THE COMPANY AND YOURSELF

PART 2: DEFINE THE CHALLENGE

PART 3: IMAGINE SUCCESS

PART 4: CREATE OPTIONS

PART 5: EVALUATE BARRIERS TO SUCCESS

PART 6: CHOOSE THE FUTURE

Chapter Topics

Separate Responsibilities—Good for You, Good for the Company

My Job Today

Strengths and Passions

Zone of Leadership

CHAPTER 2

YOUR ZONE OF LEADERSHIP
You are not the company. Choose your own future.

As the leader of your company, you have two responsibilities. You are responsible for the company. And you are responsible for yourself. Both are important, and they are different.

When using *Create the Future* to make crucial decisions for the company, separate your responsibilities for yourself and your responsibilities for the company.

You are not the company.

The thesis of this chapter is to be open about your responsibility for yourself and your family while also taking full responsibility for the organization you lead. Being open about your personal responsibilities does not conflict with your responsibilities for the organization you lead and will strengthen your leadership role.

This chapter is a guide for finding the professional role that best matches your Strengths and your Passions.

The chapter topics are:

Separate Responsibilities—Good for You, Good for the Company
You have dual responsibilities as a company leader and as an individual. Care and advocacy for both are good for the company and good for you.

My Job Today
Start your assessment of your path forward by profiling your job today.

Strengths and Passions
Knowing your Strengths and Passions establishes the guidelines for finding your best-fit job.

Zone of Leadership

Your Zone of Leadership is where your Strengths and Passions intersect.

This chapter includes three exercises identifying your Strengths and Passions and profiling your Zone of Leadership. They are valuable tools at any point in your career. The exercises draw on open public resources. If you have the budget and time to work with a coach or a career planning service, those resources will build on your work in this chapter.

Taking time to clarify how your Strengths and Passions match your job today and explore your professional path forward is a confidence-building exercise. Profiling your Zone of Leadership and defining your ideal Zone of Leadership Job do not mean you are getting ready to leave your current job and are looking for a new job. The exercises will help you understand yourself better and prepare you for your role in your current organization or any organization.

Review this chapter and select the parts helpful for you at this point in your journey. You may want to do each exercise and compile notes, beginning with your job today and ending with your ideal Zone of Leadership Job. Or you could pull two or three topics from the exercises and discuss them with a close friend. Put at least some of what you are thinking and learning in writing, even if you do not keep your notes long term. You will capture more of what you learn if you write it down. And your most creative moments may be lost if you do not record at least the highlights of your thinking and what you hear from others.

You may be adept at separating your personal and professional responsibilities and have a clear vision of your job and your nonprofessional life over the next few years. If that is where you are, skip this chapter. If you want to examine your career and life path, this chapter gives you the tools to do that.

Learn from the Experiences of Others

The analysis and exercises in this chapter are for you to do by yourself. If you can make it work, I recommend that after you do these exercises, you meet with trusted advisors. Learn about their experiences in circumstances similar to yours.

I belong to a peer support group of business leaders. When I need help with professional or personal issues, I ask them to share their experiences with similar problems. They do not know as much about me as I do, and they do not know the complexity of my situation. But they do know about their own experiences. I learn insights I would never have drawn from my experiences as I listen to them describe their life experiences. I can often apply these approaches to the issues I face.

Sharing challenges in my life with trusted advisors and learning from their experiences are the basis for my recommendation that you take a risk. Find several people whose counsel you trust. Join a peer support group like Vistage or the Young Presidents' Organization (YPO). Share the issues you are working through and ask about their experiences. Listen and learn. Talking with someone you trust who knows you well will enrich your understanding of what you are going through. Even if you are working with a professional coach, find one or two trusted advisors with whom you can share your professional experiences.

After each conversation, write brief notes on what you heard and learned—new ideas and conflicting ideas. Listen to how you talk about the topics when discussing them with different people. By listening to what you are saying, you will learn more about your own thinking.

For an introduction to peer support groups, scan the QR code that follows to read the *Harvard Business Review* article "How to Get the Most Out of Peer Support Groups."

SEPARATE RESPONSIBILITIES
—GOOD FOR YOU, GOOD FOR THE COMPANY

You could be the company owner or a production line supervisor. You could

Share the issues you are working through with a peer support group or trusted personal advisors and ask about their experiences. Listen and learn.

---

be a sergeant in the Army or president of the United States. You are responsible for your personal life, and you are responsible for the welfare and future of your platoon, your production line section, your department, your company, and your country.

Each of us has dual responsibilities for ourselves and the organizations we lead. Dual responsibilities are part of life.

Whatever your title or role, making decisions on behalf of a corporation, a nonprofit, a government agency, or an educational institution is your responsibility. In some situations, the decisions will impact you personally. Even in those cases, your obligation is to act in the overall interest of the organization. Leaders get in trouble when they confuse their desires for themselves with their responsibilities for the company.

If I am an investor or an employee, I want you, as the leader, to make decisions for the benefit of the company and not simply for your personal interest. I also want your professional and personal goals to be aligned with the company's success. I want you to believe that you are the best person to lead the company and that leading the company is the best place for you at this point in your career. When you are in a job that is a good match with your Strengths and Passions, you are the right person for the job, and the job is right for you.

Responsibility does not mean you have complete control over what happens to the organization. But the vision you create, the decisions you make, the questions you ask, the goals you set, the insights you offer, and the extra effort you make will create the future for the organization.

Before engaging with the CTF Team to identify potential paths forward for the company, both you and the company will benefit from your being clear about where you are at this point in your professional career and what professional role is the best expression of your Zone of Leadership. At some phases in your career, a challenging job with high risks is an OK place to be.

Starting a new company with rewards later if you are successful is an example. Being challenged is how you will learn and grow. Other times, a lower-risk job executing on your core competencies is right. Getting clear about where you can be successful and what is best for you at this point in your career is the idea.

You may want to change your role in the company. You may want to retire. You may see opportunities to grow the company but do not believe you have the skills or want to lead the larger company. The company may require cost reductions, and you don't want to be the one to make the cuts.

In cases like this, getting clarity about your motivations and personal goals will strengthen your leadership as you decide the company's future.

If your job is a good match with your Strengths, your Passions, and the current phase in your career, you will be in your Zone of Leadership. You will be more successful, and you will be happier. And the company will be more successful. A leader who does not have the needed skills or is unhappy doing the job is bad for the company.

During a conversation I had with the owner of a textile company in Henan Province in China, he said, "My business is my life." His decisions for the company were also decisions for his life and his family. Textile company owners in Milan, Italy, or Greensboro, North Carolina, will use the same words. The Henan Province company owner thinks of the business as his life. But he is making decisions for six hundred employees, suppliers in Australia, and customers in China, Europe, and the United States.

The Henan Province company owner will make better decisions for the company and, by extension, for himself and his family if he first works through where he is at this phase of his life and what he wants from his professional life and his personal life.

Financial security could be his personal goal. Or, reducing the amount of time he is working for the company could be his goal. There is no right or

---

When you are in a job that is a good match with your Strengths and Passions, you are the right person for the job, and the job is right for you.

wrong answer. Just because the company could grow does not mean growing the company is the right choice for this owner. Separating his decisions for the company from his decisions for himself and his family is difficult. After years of working to create and grow the company, moving from "my business is my life" to "I am not the textile company" is difficult to do.

If you are in a position similar to the textile company owner, consider what you want the next phase of your career to be like for you and your family. Then make decisions for the company that are right for the company and also allow your life to move in the direction that is best for you.

You may decide that "my business is my life" is what you want. You may decide that you want to lead the company through its next growth phase while also carving out time for yourself and your family. Or you might decide that you are not the right person to lead the company going forward and that you want to spend your time doing other things. You could sell the company or bring on new leadership. Each of these different paths forward can be valid. The path for the company and the path for yourself are choices you have and decisions you must make. You will be better prepared to make these decisions when you know your Zone of Leadership.

Jeff, a longtime business associate, was the "hired-hand" CEO of a U.S.-based company making sophisticated displays for the military. The company's board believed they could sell their displays to the consumer virtual reality market. The board wanted a CEO who would take the company through the long technical and market transition to civilian products. Jeff was doubtful their expensive displays could be adapted to consumer products and did not want to make that lengthy commitment. He worked with the board as they hired a new CEO who was fully engaged with the board's plans for the company.

Bracken Darrell, CEO of Logitech in California, talks about "firing yourself." When I spoke with him about this approach, he acknowledged that experience is valuable—you don't know what you don't know without experience. But he also sees a "newcomer's advantage." Darrell recommends that every leader "fire" themselves occasionally and write a description for their job. Taking that approach brings the newcomer's point of view to the specifications for the job as it is today.

The Fire Yourself approach encourages you to look at what skills the person in the job you hold today must have to be successful. "What skills do I need

What skills do I need to be the right person for the position I hold today? How should I be spending my time?

to be the right person for the position I hold today? How should I be spending my time?" As a result, you may adjust how you are doing your job. Or you and the company may be stronger if you are in a different role.

MY JOB TODAY

Either explicitly or implicitly, you will do CTF within the framework of who you are and your plans for your career. The first of three exercises described in this chapter, Exercise 2-1, "My Job Today," establishes a baseline statement describing your current job, your distinctive contributions, and the influences of the job on your personal life. No right or wrong answers. Just the facts as you see them.

Most people will take a couple of hours by themselves to outline their job profile or just think about the exercise. Making notes to record your thinking is the best approach. Use a brief outline format. Record basic ideas and not a long memo.

My Job Today

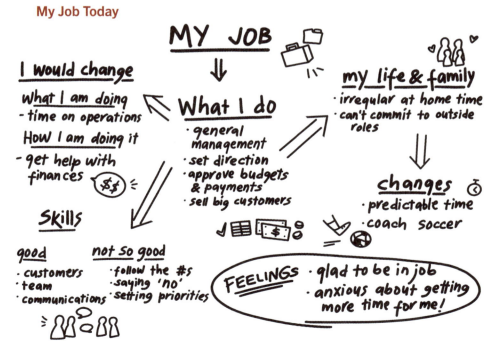

Exercise 2-1
My Job Today

This exercise profiles your job and your job's impact on your non-work life. Describe your role, but put the most thought into your contributions, shortcomings, and life experiences driven by the job.

Exercise Steps

- ▶ Describe your special skills and contributions.
- ▶ Describe your weaknesses or shortcomings in performing your current job.
- ▶ Identify elements of your personal and family life materially controlled or influenced by the requirements of your job.
- ▶ Identify elements of your personal and family life materially controlled or influenced by how you do your job.
- ▶ Identify requirements of the job materially controlling or influencing your personal or family life that you would change if you could.

Exercise Work Product

- ▶ My Job Today Profile identifying your special strengths and weaknesses and your job's impact on your personal and family life

> You will be most successful—in a job, on a sports team, or in a marriage—when your personal strengths are important to that role and when you are passionate about what you are doing.

If you have a spouse, close friend, or peer support group with whom you can share your thinking, ask for their experiences with similar issues after completing the exercise. Write a summary of what you are learning from the experiences of others. Revise your exercise notes with new insights. The results of this exercise and others in this chapter are for your personal use and do not go in the Decision Book.

STRENGTHS AND PASSIONS

Start by knowing yourself.

You will be most successful—in a job, on a sports team, or in a marriage—when your personal strengths are important to that role and when you are passionate about what you are doing. Putting yourself in positions where your strengths are valuable and you realize your passions is the goal of your Zone of Leadership work.

Much has been written about leadership, setting goals, and character. A *Harvard Business Review* article titled "The Founder's Dilemma" by Noam Wasserman is particularly relevant for this discussion. "The Founder's Dilemma" is credited with the concept of "Do you want to be rich, or do you want to be king?" Wasserman summarized the research showing that the motivation of a company founder profoundly influences the company's outcome and the founder's financial success. Company founders more influenced by a desire to maintain control (be king) have lower financial rewards than founders who are willing to give up control to allow the company to grow.

Being rich or being king are not the only motivational options for your career. Proving you are right, meeting parental expectations, curing cancer that disabled your child, or continuing a family tradition could be your motivation. Understanding your motivations will lead to better decisions for yourself and your company and is core to being an authentic leader.

Most of us can quickly and superficially answer the question, "What are you passionate about?" We are passionate about our kids, our sports team, and our spouse. Some of us will have a cause or life passion expressed in our work or pastime activities. Passion as a motivation for our professional career is a complex topic most of us do not understand well.

Passion Examples
- Motivation
- Aspiration
- Compassion

Defining skills relevant to your career can also be challenging. Beyond knowing how to do a specific task, your non-knowledge skills are often primary determinants of the roles in which you can be successful.

Strength and Skill Examples
- Knowledge
- Communications
- Empathy
- Grit

Exercise 2-2, "Strengths and Passions," defines your strengths and passions. As you go through the exercise, think broadly about things you have done that you felt passionate about doing, and think about skills you have demonstrated in any part of your life. Your Zone of Leadership is the intersection of your passions and your strengths—tasks or jobs you do that pull from both.

This exercise develops a profile of your Strengths and Passions—a top-line profile and not a deep-dive personality evaluation. The resulting profile identifies your Strengths and Passions and the principal drivers of your professional career. The profile becomes the touchstone for defining the job or role in which you will excel.

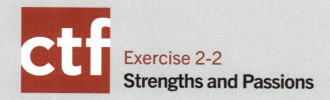

Exercise 2-2
Strengths and Passions

This exercise develops a profile of your strengths and passions using online survey instruments. Take the tests after reviewing the instructions. With the results in hand, profile your concept of achievement and success.

Exercise Steps

▶ Scan the QR code that follows or visit *store.gallup.com/c/en-us/1/cliftonstrengths* to take the Strengths survey.

▶ List knowledge strengths, personal characteristics, and work practices you believe are strengths. Based on the survey results, list your top five strengths.
▶ Scan the QR code that follows or visit *viacharacter.org/survey/account/register* to take the Passions survey.

▶ List your top five Passions.
▶ Describe what achievement means to you.
▶ Describe what success means to you.

Exercise Work Products
- My Strengths
- My Passions
- My Motivations in terms of success and achievement

Complete the exercise by writing a keyword profile of your Strengths, Passions, and Motivations. Put your notes down for several days. Talk to trusted advisors, if possible. Think about what you have learned about yourself and what you have heard from others. Go back to your profile and revise or clarify if needed.

My Strengths and Passions

My Profile

Strengths
- Achiever
- Strategic
- Futuristic
- Learner
- Analytical

Passions
- Judgments
- Curiosity
- Creativity
- Zest
- Bravery

ZONE OF LEADERSHIP

Having profiled your Strengths and Passions, you can now find your Zone of Leadership. Your job is in your Zone of Leadership when it expresses your Passions and uses your Strengths. You may also want to develop a profile of your next job or career path expressing your aspirations and your Strengths and Passions. This profile will be your Zone of Leadership Job. We usually don't get everything we want or hope for in life, but knowing where we are today and where we want to go will bring us closer to our preferred life experience.

The company founder or CEO who loves working with customers and hates "running the company" is the classic example of a leader who should

Your job is in your Zone of Leadership when it expresses your Passions and uses your Strengths.

---

separate operations management functions from his job. With a Chief Operating Officer (COO) "running the company," the CEO will be happier, and the company will be more successful.

We see the reverse story too often. The company is doing well with a primarily externally focused CEO working with an internally focused COO. The CEO moves to another company or retires. The COO knows the company and is seen as the low-risk choice for CEO. After a year or two, the company is not doing well. The person with the title of CEO was a great COO. That was his Zone of Leadership. He does not like being the external guy for the company and is not good in that role.

Promoting the best salesperson to be the sales manager often has the same result. We hear this story in the context of the "Peter principle," where employees are promoted to their level of incompetence. Aligning the job and its requirements with your team member's Zone of Leadership is a better way of building an effective team. Find the person who will be a good sales manager rather than "rewarding" the best salesperson by promoting them to sales manager.

There are no good or bad people in these stories. Things go wrong when we put good people in positions of responsibility that do not align with their Strengths and Passions.

The Venn diagram overlap of activities expressing both your Strengths and Passions is your Zone of Leadership. Exercise 2-3, "Zone of Leadership," starts with your Strengths and Passions and identifies your Zone of Leadership. Your Zone of Leadership is a target profile of where you will be most successful and where you will be "happy" doing what you are doing.

Your "ideal job" profile—a Zone of Leadership Job—becomes your guide for your professional career planning. The profile is also a tool for communicating who you are to others and describing roles in which you will be most impactful. If staying in your current job is the best place for you over the next few years, your Zone of Leadership Job profile becomes a guide as you adjust your role in the company to bring it more in line with your Zone of Leadership Job.

Exercise 2-3
Zone of Leadership

This exercise identifies activities you are doing, have done, or could do using your Strengths and your Passions. The Venn diagram overlap of activities expressing both your Strengths and Passions is your Zone of Leadership. You then profile the ideal job in your Zone of Leadership.

Exercise Steps

- Identify activities you have done or are doing that express your Strengths.
- Identify activities expressing your Passions.
- From the Strength and Passion activities, write a separate list of activities you are doing or have done that express BOTH your Strengths and your Passions.
- Write a separate list of activities you believe you can do that express BOTH your Strengths and your Passions.
- Drawing from the two lists of activities you believe express both your Strengths and your Passions, outline or describe your Zone of Leadership—activities using your Strengths and expressing your Passions.
- Based on the activities you believe are the best match to your Zone of Leadership, prepare a job description of your ideal Zone of Leadership Job that is realistically achievable in two to five years.

Exercise Work Products

- Definition of your Zone of Leadership
- Profile of your ideal Zone of Leadership Job

Things go wrong when we put good people in positions of responsibility that do not align with their Strengths and Passions.

Keep in mind your comments on the impact of your job on your personal and family life from Exercise 2-1. Ideally, you want to be happy in your job and at home. When doing work like this, I usually take my thinking further when I let my answers percolate for a few days. I go back to the answers—clarify and revise.

> *The idea that your dream job already exists . . . is a fairy tale. You design your "really pretty terrific and surprisingly close to a dream" job the same way you design your life—by thinking like a designer, by generating options, by prototyping, and by making the best choices possible.*
> —Bill Burnett and Dave Evans, *Designing Your Life*

Zone of Leadership

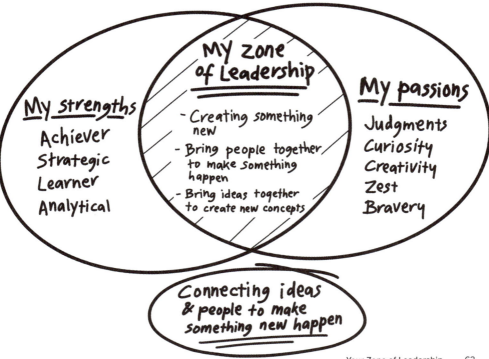

After completing these exercises, you will better understand your aspirations, motivations, and skills. You will have a profile of the professional role best matched to your Zone of Leadership. As you lead or participate in the CTF work for the company, you can and will be able to:

- More confidently separate your responsibilities to the company from your responsibilities to yourself and your family
- Challenge yourself and other participants in the CTF work to find creative future options for the company, independent of your concerns for your own career path
- Be more successful in removing your personal agenda from your thinking about the company's welfare
- More clearly focus your decision-making on the company's welfare

Whatever decisions you and other leaders make for the company, you will have a vision of your path forward. Usually, that will be as part of the company leadership. But you will have thought about where you are in your professional career and better understand what professional roles best express your skills and passions. I include a more in-depth description of the process for finding your Zone of Leadership in my companion book, *Create the Future—the Workbook*.

The Zone of Leadership concept was developed by Bernard Heine, Professional Business Coaches, Inc., building on work by Harvard professor Tal Ben-Shahar. Scan the QR code that follows or visit *theprofessionalbusinesscoaches.com/get-into-your-leadership-zone* for more information.

KEY TAKEAWAYS
1. You are not the company.
2. Knowing yourself is essential to being an effective leader.
3. Your Zone of Leadership is where your passions and personal strengths overlap.
4. When you are in a job that is a good match with your Strengths and Passions, you are the right person for the job, and the job is right for you.

PART 1: PREPARE THE COMPANY AND YOURSELF

▼

PART 2: DEFINE THE CHALLENGE

▼

PART 3: IMAGINE SUCCESS

▼

PART 4: CREATE OPTIONS

▼

PART 5: EVALUATE BARRIERS TO SUCCESS

▼

PART 6: CHOOSE THE FUTURE

Chapter Topics

Your Motivation for Using CTF

Your Leadership Statement

Leadership Roles

CHAPTER 3

THE LEADER'S ROLE
Decision Maker, Leader of the Company, and Team Leader.

What do you hope to get from your investment in CTF? And why should someone care about the company's future and what you hope to accomplish?

Your homework assignment answering these questions begins this chapter. You will get more value from your investment in CTF if you set goals for yourself and have a rationale for this effort that goes beyond the benefits to you. This chapter also profiles three leadership roles you and others will play that are integral to the Create the Future process.

The chapter topics are:

Your Motivation for Using CTF
Begin by outlining your goals for the CTF work. Profile the benefits you expect for the company and for yourself.

Your Leadership Statement
To get value from the CTF Team's work, you must have a purpose for their work that is meaningful to them.

Leadership Roles
I profile the roles of Decision Maker, Leader of the Company, and Team Leader/Facilitator in the CTF process.

YOUR MOTIVATION FOR USING CTF
Your reasons for using CTF could be: You are excited by the potential you see in your company but are not sure how to exploit the opportunity you imagine.

Whatever your motivation for using the Create the Future approach to discovery and decision-making, be clear what you hope to accomplish for yourself and for the company you lead.

Or, your company is in trouble with declining sales, and you want help improving its prospects or capturing what value is left. Or you want to launch a new product and need board approval for the investment. Your feelings could range from "I am afraid and don't know what to do" to "I know exactly what to do, and I need to get my board to understand what I am trying to do."

Whatever your motivation for using the Create the Future approach to discovery and decision-making, be clear what you hope to accomplish for yourself and for the company you lead.

Exercise 3-1, "Your Motives for Using CTF," is your guide for clarifying and recording your reasons for using CTF. You will work through what you hope to get from your efforts and from the Team's participation. You will also create a list of decisions you and other Deciders must make. This list will be your contribution when the Team develops the Decision Agenda in Chapter 11. Create the Future Thinking's creative, disciplined, and systematic process for outlining your goals for using CTF and the decisions you must make will get you better results than a more informal, instinctive approach.

Reserve time by yourself to think about the exercise questions. Write out your answers. Writing the answers is important. Put them down for a few days. Review your thinking. Revise, clarify, and simplify your answers.

Your answers to these exercise questions are for your personal use and guidance. Keep the answers in your personal file. The results should not go in the Decision Book unless your CTF Team is you and one or two other company founders or owners. If your company has a board of directors that makes final decisions and you are the CEO, share a summary of your thinking with the board before they begin the CTF work.

You could use the following CTF exercises as a guide for your thinking rather than involving others. If you take that approach, get away by yourself.

Turn off your cell phone, and don't check your email. Do the exercises on sheets of paper or a whiteboard. Think about where the company could go and the life you want to be living going forward.

Innovative leaders, like Steve Jobs, sometimes take giant steps forward without the constraints of advisors. Some of Jobs's innovations worked, and some did not. The challenge each of us faces is knowing ourselves and choosing the best decision-making process for ourselves and the problem before us at this moment in time.

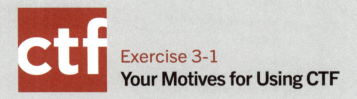

Exercise 3-1
Your Motives for Using CTF

Begin your Create the Future work by getting clear about your motives and your goals for the CTF discovery and decision-making process.

Exercise Steps
Write keyword answers to each question. Then use those keywords to write a summary of your motivation for using CTF.
- What do you hope to accomplish by using CTF?
- What do you hope CTF will do for you as leader of your organization?
- How do you believe CTF will help your leadership team?
- How do you believe CTF will benefit the company?
- How do you believe CTF will benefit the company's owners?
- What do you see as your role in the CTF work?
- What decisions must you and other Decision Makers make that will be influenced by the CTF work?

Exercise Work Products
- Statement of your motivation for using CTF and your goals for the work
- Leader's Initial Decisions to Be Made Statement

Your Motivation for Using CTF

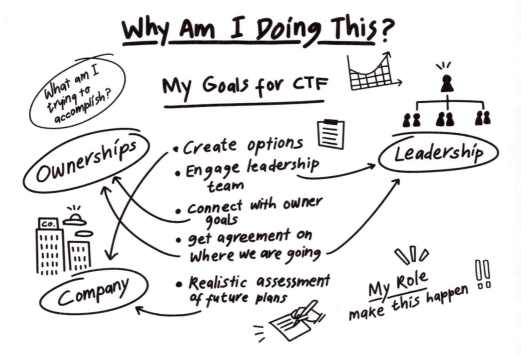

YOUR LEADERSHIP STATEMENT

Before asking someone who is not a paid consultant to help you choose a future path for the company, ask yourself, "Why should they care?"

When you talk to someone about joining the Team, answering the "Why should I care?" question will be an important part of the conversation. You may compensate outside advisors who join the Team, but their pay rate will probably be less than a professional consultant's fee. You want all Team members to give careful thought to the recommendations they make. You want them to care about the future of the company and their role as part of the Team. Simply making you wealthier or more successful will not be motivating to them.

Don't ask anyone to participate until you can simply and clearly, think elevator pitch, communicate the problem you want their help solving and why they should be interested in the company's future. Your job is to create a vision for the CTF work and the company's future that is meaningful to those you are asking to help you.

The Team could be your "leadership team," board of directors, executive committee, advisory board, or an advisory group you create. Whatever the composition of the CTF Team, the members will put more into their participation and be more engaged with the issues you are raising if they see the issues as relevant, important, or interesting to them.

The first reaction of many when they hear about a "planning meeting" is, "I don't want to spend another minute in a planning meeting that will change nothing!" You will be committing your time, and you will ask others to commit their time. To get full engagement by the Team members, you must convince them that their work will be an essential contribution to determining the company's future.

You can use *Create the Future*'s five steps as a personal guide for making better decisions. The Team exercises can be checklists for your exploration of the issues. Or you can work with a Team and take them through the CTF exercises. A Team will bring different perspectives into the exploration and decision-making process and strengthen your role as leader and Decision Maker.

Exercise 3-2, "Your Leadership Statement," is your guide for creating a description of the Problem and a concept of Success. These become your elevator pitch. Before asking busy professionals to help you, define the Problem, create a vision of Success, and compose a rationale for their participation in your initiative. Your homework assignment from this chapter is to write a simple statement explaining why the company's welfare is important to those you are asking to join the Team and perhaps the broader community of those impacted by the company. Answer the question, "Why should I care what happens to this company?" from the perspective of the company's employees, customers, suppliers, investors, and community. The answer may not be the same for each, but there will be common themes.

As with your My Motivation notes, your Leader's Statements are for your personal use and guidance. Save your exercise answers in your personal file, and do not include them in the Decision Book.

Before asking someone to help you choose a future path for the company, ask yourself, "Why should they care?"

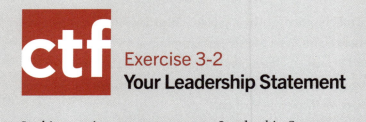

Exercise 3-2
Your Leadership Statement

In this exercise, you prepare your Leadership Statement summarizing the Problem facing the company and a vision of Success. You also prepare a rationale for why the company's future should matter to CTF Team members.

Exercise Steps
Write keyword answers to each question. Then write summaries of the Problem, Success, and Why You Should Care.
- The Problem: What is the opportunity or threat facing the company?
- Success: What would success look like?
- Why should I care? Why does the future of this company matter?
  » as an employee
  » as a customer
  » as an investor
  » as a government or public entity
  » as a community or society
- Write a simple statement about why the organization's future is important.
- Write a simple statement about why the Create the Future work is important.

Exercise Work Products
- The Problem—The Leader's Statement
- Success—The Leader's Statement
- Why You Should Care—Elevator Pitch for the company and CTF

Preparing your Motivation and Goals statements will clarify your thinking about the company's future. When the Team convenes, it will create a Problem Statement, a Success Statement, a Vision Statement, and an Operational Goals Statement. Your thinking will be a guide for the Team. But let the Team create its own Statements and own the Statements. The results of the Team's work will be a shared vision of where the company is going.

It's Your Company. You Decide.

Consider the challenge for Girardino. He is the fourth-generation leader of a custom glass fabrication company on the island of Murano in Venice, Italy. Their blue glass vases are sold through high-end distributors in Europe and North America. The company is stable but under pressure from lower-cost glass products from China. Girardino wants to use the CTF exercises to help him decide where to take the company. He plans to ask several long-term staff members, two family members, and three outside advisors to join the CTF Team.

Many company employees have spent their entire working careers making glass vases for Girardino's family. But they do not own the company. Staff and advisors could say, "This is your company. You figure it out and decide."

If Girardino wants to have a creative and energetic discussion of the company's future, he must have a rationale as to why Team members should care about the future of the company. Girardino must give them a reason to care that is meaningful to them.

It matters whether the goal of the Team's work will be to make more money for Girardino and his family or to save the company, staff jobs, and keep high-end glassmaking as a vital part of the Venetian economy. Before asking others to join the Team, Girardino needs to put himself in the shoes of the Team members and imagine why they might care about the company's future and the Team's work.

Why Should They Care?

LEADERSHIP ROLES

Three leadership roles are important to the CTF process: the Decision Maker; the Company Leader; and the Team Leader (or the facilitator of the Team). Each is an essential leadership role, and they are different. You may serve in one or more of these roles. Take a moment to review the particular responsibilities of each leader and their role in the CTF process.

Decision Maker

A Decision Maker's responsibilities are to contribute, to learn, and to decide.

The Decision Maker could be the CEO, the board/executive committee, or the company owner. In the CTF context, the Decision Maker is the one who will make the final choices about where the organization will go. The Decision Maker's role is complex because she is both the client of the Team and a contributor to the Team. The Decision Maker sets goals and expectations for the CTF work and participates as a Team member.

Believing you can imagine and choose the future for your company is at the core of the Create the Future approach. Take a moment to think about what these beliefs mean to you and your role as a Decision Maker. Think through how you will talk about your beliefs with the Team and what your expectations will be from the Team in terms of their contributions and participation in the process. Think through how you will talk about your role as a Team member while also being a Decider.

Successful leaders are both decisive and vulnerable. They are open to hearing other points of view and are prepared to make decisions. The Decision Maker participates as a Team member when the Team develops information, offers alternative points of view, and clarifies the options under consideration. The Decision Maker must welcome the Team's views and contributions and also be clear that she will make the final calls. These two messages are fundamental to CTF.

You want the Team to challenge conventional thinking, unexpressed assumptions, and your own beliefs. Even when the only participants are Deciders, the two mindsets of "I am open to new ideas" and "I will decide" must both be present. The cases of a young company with three founders or a larger company where the board of directors is the Team come to mind. In both situations, the Deciders will say, "Put our Decider's hats in the closet. Let's figure out what we are trying to accomplish and what options we have for where we could take this company." When the time comes to choose the path forward, the Deciders will say, "Time to put our Decider's hats back on and decide."

Human nature and normal dynamics within an organization encourage your staff, your board, and your consultants to look for signals from you about what you want. Encourage the Team to speak its mind, to take risks, and to believe that you are open to other points of view. This approach will create more options and opportunities.

Successful leaders are both decisive and vulnerable. They are open to hearing other points of view and are prepared to make decisions.

You will miss an opportunity to discover an even better idea, strategy, or market opportunity if you are closed to learning about other options and points of view—even when, in your mind, the value of CTF is bringing your board and other stakeholders up to speed with your vision.

Consider the predictably different outcomes Felipe—the owner of an Orlando, Florida-based company that finds low-cost jet charters for leisure travel—will get from different approaches he could take to engage with his leadership team on new growth initiatives. Felipe's business has plateaued, and he believes moving from the leisure travel market to the high-end business travel market will build revenues and profits.

Suppose he pulls his leadership team together to go through the CTF exercises and begins the meeting by saying he wants to move the company into business travel. In that case, the suggestions he is likely to hear from the Team will relate to charters for business travel. Team members will not risk putting alternatives forward that conflict with his preconceived point of view.

Alternatively, Felipe could say his goal is to grow the company, and he is looking for ways to do that. One option is moving into business travel, but he wants to consider others. If he takes a more open approach, a Team member might suggest moving from selling hours on a charter jet to selling a high-end travel experience built around the jet charters. With several opportunities for growth on the table, Felipe's chances of finding a growth initiative the company can successfully implement will be higher.

Leader of the Company

The primary responsibility of the Leader of the Company is to represent "the company" in the CTF discussions, to represent CTF to the company, and to keep the company moving forward while CTF is underway.

You could be the owner of the company and the president. You could be a hired-hand CEO serving at the board's pleasure. In both cases, you are the Leader of the Company. You will be the primary communicator about CTF to the company, set expectations and norms, and represent the company as a whole in the reality-check exercises.

Communication about Create the Future

As Leader of the Company, you will be responsible for telling the company and the outside world about CTF. You will be the ambassador of CTF to the company. Even though the CTF work will be confidential, people outside the Team will know something about the work. How the CTF initiative is communicated to the staff is your responsibility during preparations for the work and while it is underway. The message to communicate may come from the Decision Makers, but you will be the messenger.

Setting norms within the Team

As Leader of the Company, you will know most Team members and be seen as "a Leader" if not "the Leader" of the Team. You will have primary responsibility for establishing norms within the Team.

Even when the Team is the company's board of directors and you are the company's CEO, you and your staff will have organized the CTF meetings. Board members will look to you for direction and "how this is supposed to work."

If you communicate ambivalence about the process and are noncommittal about the value of the Team's work, the Team will also be ambivalent and non-committable. The messaging you send by what you say and by how you participate will establish the norm for other Team members.

Also, think about how your style works within the CTF process. You may see yourself as the driver of innovation who wants a central role in getting new ideas on the table. You may want to stay more removed from the dialogue and listen to ideas before committing yourself. Or you may see yourself as the primary source of challenge questions intended to bring out what people are thinking but not saying. Get the most value from the CTF process by building on your style as a leader.

As an example, consider the Company Leader's role when the head of sales makes what might be an unrealistic suggestion for a new product. You

Get the most value from the CTF process by building on your style as a leader.

---

are the CEO leading the Team meeting Friday morning in Liverpool in the UK. Accepting different points of view and constructively bringing contrary opinions to the table is essential. Ralph, the Director of Sales, suggests using the company's LED lighting technology in automobile headlights, building on their capability to change color under different lighting conditions. Tommy, the Manufacturing Director, responds, "That's a dumb idea. You sales guys are always promising products we don't make and probably can't make."

Edward is an outside facilitator for the meeting. The Team looks to you as CEO for a signal. Are Tommy's comments within CTF norms? Edward might step in. If not, a short statement from you is needed to establish expectations. "Ralph, interesting idea. Is there a market for color-tunable car headlights, and can we get into the market? Tommy, I want to hear your thoughts on whether we could make the lights, but let's learn about Ralph's idea first."

Encourage the risk-takers like Ralph. Also, encourage the reality-checkers like Tommy while coaching them on how to make positive statements. "All ideas are good ideas, and we are all in this together," may sound like singing "Kumbaya." But the Team can have strong give-and-take while moving forward together.

Bring reality to the discussion

The CTF exercises ask the Team to imagine future options for the company. The Team also assesses the company's realistic potential for success with each option—each Choice for the Future. "Can we really do that?" is the question the Leader of the Company must be sure is asked in the execution barriers work of Chapter 9.

The CEO will understand the capabilities and limitations of the company as a whole and will have some understanding of each department. The Team in Liverpool had the Directors of Sales and Manufacturing in the room. They will know more about capabilities and limitations in their departments than the CEO.

If an outside facilitator is leading the meeting, the CEO will know more about the company's operations than the facilitator. The CEO must let the facilitator run and maintain control of the meeting. But when the CEO sees the team has not offered an important reality check on a proposal, the CEO must start the reality-check discussion. "Ralph, is there any market intelligence suggesting there is demand for color-tunable headlights?" If Tommy is not offering comments on whether the color-tunable lights can be manufactured, the CEO must ask Tommy to put that information on the board.

The CEO also understands the connections within the company. An option on the whiteboard could require investing in marketing and sales for two years with a resulting drop in EBITDA (earnings before taxes, interest, depreciation, and amortization). The CEO is the one who must make the connection to possibly violating loan covenants or missing investor expectations.

Team Leader and Facilitator

The prime responsibility of the Team Leader is to organize the CTF work and drive it through to a conclusion.

To be a valuable resource to the company and its leadership, the Team itself must have leadership. The Team Leader is either a Decider or is acting with the authority of the Decider. The Team Leader could be the CEO, owner of the company, a senior staff member, or a consultant/facilitator working on behalf of the Decision Maker.

The owner of a smaller company who wants to engage advisors to help him figure out where to take the company will probably be the Team Leader working with an assistant. A larger company CEO will probably delegate the Team leadership to a senior staff member with relevant experience and hire an outside consultant to plan the Team meetings and be a facilitator.

The Team Leader needs to decide well before the first meeting what role he or she will play and who will facilitate the meeting. Some people are comfortable facilitating the discussion and being the person at the whiteboard. Others are not. Think about who is the best member of the Team to be at the board encouraging dialogue and capturing key ideas. If an outside facilitator is hired, that role can be limited to meeting facilitation or can include many of the Team Leader's coordination tasks. In most circumstances, the Decider should not be the meeting facilitator. If you, the Decider, are not facilitating the Team meeting, the Team's contributions will be more freely offered, and you will have more time to understand and consider the Team's contributions.

The responsibilities of the Team Leader and a facilitator working with the Leader are:

- Form and prepare the Team.
- Prepare a meeting schedule and select the Team exercises.
- Plan the meetings including an agenda and information packets for members before each meeting.
- Conduct the meetings.
- Record meeting notes.
- Prepare the exercise work products for inclusion in the Decision Book.
- Compile and maintain the Decision Book.
- Prepare the Decision Package.

The Team Leader will select the exercises most relevant to the decisions to be made. If the Leader is not the Decider, the Leader will work with the Decider to recruit Team members. The work product of most CTF meetings will be notes on flip charts or a whiteboard capturing the Team's contributions. The Leader will photograph these notes. Often, they will need to be cleaned up and elaborated upon to capture and fully preserve the Team's contributions. Printed copies will be assembled in the Decision Book. The Team Leader will also prepare a Decision Package profiling the decisions to be made for the Decision Makers' final meeting to choose the path forward.

KEY TAKEAWAYS

1. Before asking someone to help you choose a future path for the company, ask yourself, "Why should they care?"
2. Successful leaders are both decisive and vulnerable. They are open to hearing other points of view and are prepared to make decisions.
3. Get the most value from the CTF process by building on your style as a leader.

PART 1: PREPARE THE COMPANY AND YOURSELF

▼

PART 2: DEFINE THE CHALLENGE

▼

PART 3: IMAGINE SUCCESS

▼

PART 4: CREATE OPTIONS

▼

PART 5: EVALUATE BARRIERS TO SUCCESS

▼

PART 6: CHOOSE THE FUTURE

Chapter Topics

The Value of a Team

The Team's Role

Who Is Doing What?

Choosing the Team

Getting the Team's Work Done

Team Objectives for Its CTF Work

CHAPTER 4

ENGAGE THE TEAM
Decision Makers and trusted advisors Create the Future together.

Making better decisions is the goal of your Create the Future work. Forming a CTF Team of trusted advisors will help you make better decisions.

Decision Makers and advisors, working together, will more comprehensively evaluate the opportunities or threats and be more creative and realistic about the Choices for the Future.

This chapter is about the CTF Team and how it works. The topics are:

The Value of a Team
Engaging a Team of advisors will benefit your company and you as a Leader. Considering advice and feedback from the Team will improve any new initiative's prospects of success.

The Team's Role
I describe the role of the CTF Team, including both Decision Makers and advisors.

Who Is Doing What?
The Team includes individuals with different responsibilities in the company and relationships with the company. This section profiles their roles as Team members.

Choosing the Team
Who should and should not be on the Team?

Getting the Team's Work Done
Most Team work is done in facilitated meetings requiring Team leadership and established norms of behavior.

Team Objectives for Its CTF Work

The Team does an exercise to set goals for its work.

Decision Book—Start the Book

The Decision Book is a resource file or document for the Team and Decision Makers. (See "Getting Started" and Chapter 12, "Prepare to Choose.") If you are the CEO or Team Leader, you may have started the Decision Book with background materials. If not, start the Decision Book with the Team meeting notes from this chapter's exercise.

THE VALUE OF A TEAM

Objections

Why should I spend my time talking to people about where this company is going when they don't know as much as I do?

I already know where I want this company to go.

The last thing we need is another planning study sitting on the bookshelf.

Benefits of a Team Approach to the Company Leader/Owner

You can use Create the Future tools and Create the Future Thinking to work through where you want to take the company on your own. If you have the final say, going it alone is an option. Involving other people who will not know as much about the company as you do may complicate things from your point of view.

You can use the CTF tools on your own, but you will lose much of the value in the CTF approach. Even if you are the only one who will choose the future of the company, your chances of success will be better if at least two trusted advisors help you.

The benefits of a team approach for you as the Company Leader/Owner include:

- ▶ You will clarify your goals.
- ▶ More ideas will get on the whiteboard.
- ▶ You will test your ideas.
- ▶ Execution barriers will be better understood.

- You will refine the decisions to be made.
- You are more likely to make the important decisions.
- You are less likely to make a big mistake.

When Lila Snyder took over as CEO of Bose Corporation, the legendary developer of high-quality sound equipment, she called her staff together in town hall meetings. "Pretending you know what to do is a dangerous thing" was her mantra.

Involving trusted advisors and listening to their insights will improve your decision-making. That benefit usually does not come from an advisor giving you a better idea. The benefit comes from questions about an assumption you had not carefully considered or a request to clarify conflicting plans that you had not completely thought through.

Engaging with your advisors will give you a better understanding of your options, and you will reduce the chance of making a big mistake. Committees generate more ideas and are also more risk-averse—less likely to make big blunders. To benefit from working with the Team, you must be open to learning from the Team. Be open to hearing other points of view while also being prepared to make decisions.

Differences—The Value of a Team

History makes clear that major contributions come from people working together and bringing very different configurations of talents and skills to the table. Some are fast calculators. Others soak up knowledge and become walking libraries. Some are doggedly persistent, sticking to a problem for months or years until they make progress on it. Others have fantastic powers of focus and concentration. Some are inspirational leaders or collaborators. Others are brilliant explainers, capable of building intellectual bridges that make it possible for newcomers to join the effort and for experts to reach new vistas. Some are highly creative, able to set forth in directions that nobody else can see. Others are methodical and logical, catching mistakes that others make and identifying loopholes in calcified wisdom. Some are slow but deep thinkers, turning ideas over and over again in their heads until they discover new connections or unlock old mysteries.

—**Jacob Barandes**
Lecturer on Physics, Co-Director of Graduate Studies for Physics, Harvard University, *Harvard Gazette*, February 19, 2020

Benefits of a Team Approach to Successful Execution

Deciding ends one leadership process and begins another. You are choosing the path forward. Bringing along the staff, board, owners, and perhaps your customers is also required for success. Involving the Team in defining the problem and finding a solution builds understanding and commitment by Team members. Team members become ambassadors to the larger community of the company.

Consider the case of Allison, CEO of an Atlanta, Georgia, company selling health and beauty products to African Americans in the Southeast United States. The largest shareholders are two family office investors with Allison, the family of the founder, and other individuals holding the balance. Allison has built a strong sales and distribution network and views that network as the company's primary asset.

Allison is considering two paths for growth:

> **Option A:** Expand the company's geographic market into the Southwest United States.
>
> **Option B:** Introduce products for the Hispanic market in the current geographic market.

One investor is pressing for a growth plan, but Allison anticipates resistance from other owners to either growth path. The company's history has been in the African American community in Atlanta. The founder's family and one of the family office investors see that heritage as the rationale for the company's existence. Allison believes she can replicate their sales and distribution system in other geographies and for other products.

Allison forms a Team to help her decide which growth path to choose, if any. The Team is her board of directors and other key advisors. Part of her motivation for forming the Team is to develop an understanding and acceptance of the company's growth options by owners with divergent points of view.

Allison believes a team approach has the following benefits:

- Enables Decision Makers to hear and understand other points of view
- Enables key individuals to feel that "At least my point of view was heard"
- Builds a shared understanding of the issues and options
- Builds understanding and acceptance of the Decision Makers' role
- Builds buy-in to the final decisions
- Develops a "We worked on this together" spirit
- Creates ambassadors to the company and the larger community for the decisions

Engaging the company's senior leadership, its board, its owners, and its trusted advisors will improve the chances of successful execution.

A BATS Meeting or a CTF Meeting

My friend Bill told me over lunch about his frustration with his boss, the division manager of a Boston-area company. With great enthusiasm, Bill's boss will announce a new initiative intended to generate new customer leads. Bill knows the idea will not work but does not say anything. Going along with what the boss wants is how the company culture works.

Eventually, the new initiative does not work. Bill hears feedback that the boss believes it did not work because Bill did not work hard enough to make it work. Bill asked me whether he should write a "that's a dumb idea" memo the next time his boss announces a project Bill knows will not work. Clearly, Bill should not write a "that's a dumb idea" memo. There is a better way for Bill to approach his boss. But what should his boss have done?

Routinely, a leader will gather staff to talk about where he wants to take the company, the department, or the football team. Many leaders use these moments to announce decisions they have already made. These are "boss announces to staff" (BATS) meetings. Bill's boss conducts BATS meetings to announce new initiatives.

An alternative to a BATS meeting is a Create the Future meeting. A CTF meeting is when the staff discusses the problem, considers possible solutions, and helps the boss consider next steps. The conversation could go like this.

Boss: I have been thinking about a new initiative to reach potential customers who are not responding to our efforts to engage with them. Let's talk through a marketing and sales approach to win over these customers.

Mary: OK, what's our problem with them?

Boss: Good question. Joe, you are running sales. What are we hearing from these customers? I have an idea we could explore, but I want to hear what you guys are thinking. And, Bill, we need you to keep us in reality land.

If Bill's boss had engaged Mary, Joe, and Bill in designing the initiative, the chances of success would be higher. And Mary, Joe, and Bill would feel ownership of the plan.

Create the Future builds on a collaborative approach used every day in countless meetings. If you are the leader, every time you start a meeting, decide whether it will be a BATS meeting or a CTF meeting—your choice will determine the meeting outcome. The results will be completely different.

The same dynamics are at work when the CEO proposes a new initiative to the board of directors. The CEO is usually the principal visionary, but "announcing" to the board is different from engaging with the board. Engagement produces better results.

Give thought to the right message for meetings where an important change or issue is on the agenda. Many times, BATS is the appropriate meeting format. Let the participants know what changes will be made, what the changes are intended to achieve, and what their roles will be. When you as the Leader and the organization you lead will benefit from drawing on the experience and points of view of the participants in the meeting, signal a different meeting—a Create the Future meeting.

THE TEAM'S ROLE

Create the Future work divides into two activities.

1. **Advising:** When the Team is advising, the full Team does the creative and questioning work.

2. **Deciding:** When decisions will be made, the Decision Makers on the Team do their work.

The distinction is essential between the Team's work as an Advisor and the Decision Maker's work as the Decider. As much as possible, the rules of "all ideas are good ideas," "respect for all," and "leave your rank at the door" should apply during creative Advising Work. When Deciders must make decisions, consensus may be a goal, but those individuals empowered to decide on behalf of the organization will choose.

▶ If all Team members are Deciders for the company, they will develop options and evaluate execution risks as a Team of advisors. When they convene to choose the path forward, they will act in their capacity as Decision Makers.

▶ If the Team has both Decision Makers and non-Decision Maker members, the entire Team will perform its advisory work. When the Decision Makers are ready to begin their deciding work, the Decision Makers will convene a separate meeting to choose the future for the company.

When the Team is doing its Advising work, preparing to make decisions is the focus. The Team Leader will prepare the Decision Book to be used as a resource by the board or owners (the Deciders) when they choose the future for the company. The content of the Decision Book is the Team's work product acting as Advisors to the Decision Makers.

If you must make an important decision TODAY, separate Advising and Deciding. Convene trusted team members and advisors. Use the CTF tools to talk through the challenge, success options, barriers, and the consequences

---

If you are the leader, every time you start a meeting, decide whether it will be a BATS (boss announces to staff) meeting or a CTF meeting—your choice will determine the meeting outcome.

of the available decision choices. Use the team exercises as your guide for the Zoom call or meeting in your conference room to prepare you to make the decision TODAY. Then, openly move to the Decision work and use the tools for deciding outlined in Chapter 13, "Choose the Future."

WHO IS DOING WHAT?

Let's begin with who is doing what. A Team can include:

- Company owners
- CEO
- Board of directors
- Senior staff
- Outside advisors
- Expert consultants

The Create the Future Team

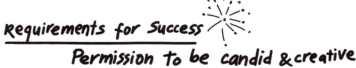

In many cases, members will play more than one Team role. You can be the Decision Maker if you own the company. If you are also the CEO, you will be the Company Leader on the Team. The roles are different in the CTF process. You must understand both roles and play both roles.

Use a non-Team member facilitator, if possible. This approach allows all Team members to fully engage with the Team's work.

The most important Team roles and responsibilities are:

TEAM ROLE	RESPONSIBILITIES
DECISION MAKER	CONTRIBUTE, LEARN, AND DECIDE.
COMPANY LEADER	REPRESENT "THE COMPANY" IN THE CTF DISCUSSIONS, REPRESENT CTF TO THE COMPANY, AND KEEP THE COMPANY MOVING AHEAD.
TEAM LEADER	ORGANIZE AND DRIVE THE CTF WORK THROUGH TO ITS CONCLUSION. PREPARE THE DECISION BOOK AND THE DECISION PACKAGE.
TEAM MEMBER	DO THE HOMEWORK, SHARE EXPERIENCES, CONTRIBUTE IDEAS, PROVIDE CANDID ADVICE, ASK QUESTIONS, AND TREAT EVERYONE AND ALL CONTRIBUTIONS WITH RESPECT.
FACILITATOR	LEAD MEETINGS, RECORD MEMBER CONTRIBUTIONS, AND COMPILE MEETING NOTES.

CHOOSING THE TEAM

Two entrepreneurs in a garage can be the Team. A larger company may have a hired hand CEO who is the Leader of the Company, a paid facilitator who is the Team Leader, and a board of directors who are the Decision Makers —the Deciders.

Individuals who are Decision Makers and who will play a material role in choosing the company's future should be participating members of the

Team. They are who they are. All other Team members should have the following characteristics:

- Ability to be a collaborator and not simply an advocate for their interests
- Openness to listening, learning, and working in an open-group process
- Willingness to commit the time
- Ability to give constructive feedback
- Diversity of experiences and perspectives

Team members will bring the Create the Future Thinking process to life—ask, discover, and learn. The personal qualities of the Team member are as important, perhaps more important, than the content of their résumé.

Team members working for the benefit of the whole company and not just themselves or their department are the best contributors. Members should be willing and able to give candid advice constructively. And Team members should be open to hearing other points of view. Decision Makers will learn from hearing different points of view and even conflicting opinions and disagreements. Advisors who simply agree with whatever the leader says are not helpful.

Deciding who should not be part of the CTF Team is as important as deciding who should be a member. Some "do not include" candidates are:

- The division director whose job is threatened by the choices to be considered
- The top salesperson who is motivated only by her next bonus check
- The R&D genius who will advocate only for funding his projects

---

The personal qualities of the Team member are as important, perhaps more important, than the content of their resume.

- Key suppliers or customers who will advocate for their company
- Your banker, lawyer, or accountant—all good people, but they will not be candid advisors
- Your golf buddy

Build the Team by starting with your board of directors, if you have one. If not, invite individuals whose advice you trust and whose experience is relevant to join the Team. From within the company, you may want to involve two or three leaders engaged in thinking about the company's future direction. Leaders of marketing, sales, and R&D are candidates if their experience and personal qualities are a fit. Including the CFO might be helpful.

Other possible additions to the CTF Team are next-generation leaders of the company. Getting their buy-in on the decisions will influence their commitment to the company, and their perspective may be a factor to consider for those making the decisions.

You want to have one or more team members who will "think outside the box." Getting crazy ideas on the whiteboard enriches the CTF work. You may not go with these ideas, but they will help you understand the full range of possibilities for the company. Some individuals can pull themes together from the scattered ideas on the whiteboard. Getting someone with those skills in the room is a plus.

Another skill to have in the room is "the realist" who will challenge the group, constructively, on the company's capabilities to execute on the proposed Future Choices. The realist may be an operations or finance person or someone in the sales organization who is not part of the senior leadership team but understands the company's capabilities.

Be sensitive to the culture of the Team and groups within the Team, such as the board of directors. Consider how explicit you will be about the contribution you expect from each member. You could say, "I want Fred to be part of this process because he understands the company and brings us back to reality." Or you may not want to pigeonhole Fred by saying that. Some teams will rotate the reality-check role or designate two people to have that role. Think through the culture, the individuals, and what you want to accomplish.

CTF Team Member Roles

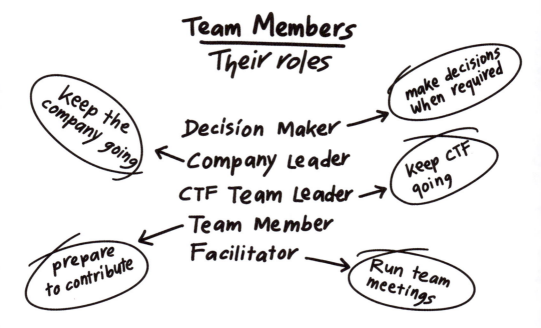

There may also be a constituency, inside or outside the company, whose involvement would be helpful. Making them advocates for, or at least neutral toward, the final decisions could be helpful. A nonconfrontational union leader might be an example. If community relations are an issue, a church leader or other civic, nonpolitical leader might be a candidate.

An "industry expert" or academic who follows business trends can be added to the Team to give perspective on the industry and where other companies are headed. You could have an expert prepare a report for the Team as background information.

You are asking Team members to take their assignment seriously and to commit their time. Unless you are asking your best friend to help you decide where to take the company, most non-employee Team members will expect compensation. You certainly will pay them if the company is larger. That cost will be a consideration when selecting the team.

Team members will see the Team's work and their participation as important if, and only if, the company leadership—the Deciders—attach importance to the work.

GETTING THE TEAM'S WORK DONE

Leadership Messages and Cultural Norms

Team members will see the Team's work and their participation as important if, and only if, the company leadership—the Deciders—attach importance to the work.

Leadership Messages

"The message must come from the top." Unless the "Leader" advocates for CTF, the rest of the company will not attach value to it. The CEO, board chair, or company owner must clearly own CTF, or it will be seen as just another planning exercise.

Leadership messages about the importance of the CTF work are essential for the Team to become a meaningful contributor. The best message from the Deciders is the combination of:

- The work we are doing is essential for determining the future of this organization.
- We will define the problem and success together as a Team.
- At the end of the CTF work, we, the Deciders, will choose the path forward for the company.

These statements communicate a determination to act and an openness to the Team's input.

Cultural Norms

Deciders and the Team Leader will establish cultural norms by how they portray the Team's work and by the expectations they set for the Team and its work. Team members will look to the Deciders and the Team Leader for how the Team works and for what is permitted and prohibited within the Team. The Deciders will establish these norms by how they participate.

Four principles guiding the Team's work are:

- What is said in the room stays in the room.
- All ideas are good ideas.
- Everyone deserves respect.
- Questioning is the path to discovery and learning.

Meeting Facilitation

When the Team is two people, such as two company owners, one person will be the recorder for the group. That person's responsibility is to capture key ideas and information in a simple, understandable format. If the group is three people or more, one person should take responsibility for managing the exercises and be the Team Leader.

The Team Leader can facilitate the meetings, but other options usually work better. If someone in the group is an effective facilitator, give them that role. Their job will be to capture all ideas and not just their ideas or ideas with which they agree. When budget funds are available, hire an outside facilitator and allow all team members to be contributors without being distracted by running the meeting and recording information on the whiteboard.

If you are the Company Leader, don't be the facilitator and notetaker. Let someone else manage the exercises, and give yourself time and space to absorb the information created by the Team.

What Not to Do

I participated as a board member in a whiteboard SWOT analysis led by the company's CEO. We were looking at four business units to decide which units were worth future investment and which were not. As we went through the analysis of each business unit, the CEO did not record much of what was being said by board members and his senior staff. The CEO had no malicious intent to suppress information. The discussion was jumping back and forth between business units with many ideas and observations. The CEO was not capturing much of what was said because he was trying to understand and evaluate each person's points.

Many valuable insights from the meeting were lost because we did not have someone at the whiteboard guiding the discussion and ensuring ideas were developed and recorded. We would have had a better outcome if an outside facilitator or another staff member was at the whiteboard whose only job was to guide the discussion and record the meeting notes.

Creating and Evaluating Choices for the Future

The CTF process puts options on the whiteboard and then does a reality check evaluating execution barriers. The creative "all ideas are good ideas" work will not happen without a clear leadership message communicating serious interest in hearing different ideas. "Check your rank and job title at the door" should be the message. You must ask some members to engage—"Bill, what do you think?" The meeting facilitator can limit the more aggressive members and encourage the more restrained. Acceptance and acknowledgment of different ideas are paramount in this phase of the CTF work.

Open and candid discussion will not happen without permission from the top. Usually, you don't need more creative people in the room. But being creative in the room must be OK.

For example, some new business models are more likely to be successful with leadership changes in key positions, including the CEO. No one on the Team will offer a leadership description for the future company that is incompatible with the current leadership unless the leader "gives permission" for that conversation. If you are that CEO, you need to be clear about what is in and out of bounds. You could say, "There may need to be changes

---

Usually, you don't need more creative people in the room. But being creative in the room must be OK.

here. What will the company need from a CEO if we go this route?" That conversation will not happen without your initiative.

A survey of staff at any organization will identify off-limit topics—such as the no-show nephew, selling the company, the pet project going nowhere, the abusive customer, and the underperforming legacy product. The Team meeting is not a gripe session to air complaints. But the Team is asked to be open and candid. When preparing for the meeting, think through what boundaries to put on the "all ideas" discussion. Set limits, but also be clear that within the discussion zone all ideas are OK. Assume uncomfortable information will not be volunteered without encouragement.

When the Team walks out of its first CTF meeting, it could be thinking:

> What a waste of time. Another dull meeting that decided nothing and went nowhere.
>
> OR
>
> That was interesting and productive. I got my views on the board, and I learned something. This might get us somewhere.

The leadership message and the Team's experience during the meeting will determine what the Team is willing to contribute and what the Team is thinking as it walks out the door. Make CTF fast and fun. Don't make it a complicated or long chore. Be clear that putting a crazy idea on the board or asking a challenging question is OK.

TEAM OBJECTIVES FOR ITS CREATE THE FUTURE WORK

Allowing Team members to talk about their goals for the Team's work and their participation is the starting point for the Team exercises. Exercise 4-1, "CTF Team Objectives for Its Work," is an opportunity for the Team to describe:

- ▸ Their goals for the Team's CTF work and its impact on the company
- ▸ Their personal goals for participation on the Team

Company Deciders, outside advisors, and key staff will participate on the Team with different interests and motivations. Even if the Team is just the company founders or a board of directors, different goals and motivations will be present. Including senior staff and outside advisors on the Team brings more diversity of views and experience to the discussion but also brings different motivations and expectations. Asking everyone to verbalize their expectations for the Team's work and their participation will make these expectations visible and reduce tensions over unexpressed motivations.

Establishing shared objectives for the Team's work and an understanding of members' motivations for participation will build confidence in the process and the Team. If establishing shared objectives is important to the Team and the decisions you must make, begin the CTF work by doing this exercise. Skip this exercise if the Team is in clear agreement on the reasons for doing CTF and the Team's role in the process.

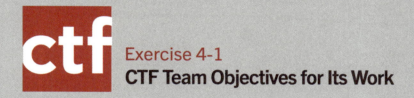

Exercise 4-1
CTF Team Objectives for Its Work

This exercise answers the question, "Why are we doing the Create the Future work?" Team members describe their objectives for the CTF work and their reasons for participating on the Team.

Exercise Steps
- Ask members what they believe the Team can contribute to addressing the company's challenge.
- Ask Team members what they believe should be the objectives or goals for the Team's work.
- Draft a consensus Team Success Statement.
- Ask each Team member to describe what they hope to get for themselves from participating in the Team's work.

Exercise Work Products
- Team Success Statement of goals for the Team's contribution to the CTF work

▸ Summary of common themes of individual members' goals for their participation on the CTF Team

Put a photo of the Team's whiteboard notes or a modestly elaborated version of the notes in the Team Meeting Notes section of the Decision Book. Create a cleaned-up and stand-alone version of the Team Success Statement and include it with the meeting notes.

Team and Member Goals for CTF

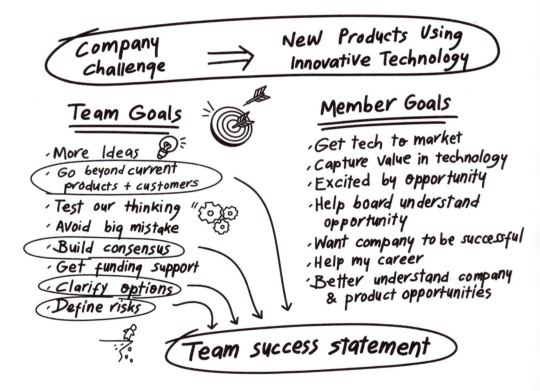

KEY TAKEAWAYS

1. Forming a CTF Team will help you make better decisions.
2. The personal qualities of the Team members are as important, perhaps more important, than the content of their résumé.
3. Usually, you don't need more creative people in the room. But being creative in the room must be OK.
4. Make CTF fast and fun. Don't make it a complicated or long chore.

PART 1: PREPARE THE COMPANY AND YOURSELF

PART 2: DEFINE THE CHALLENGE

PART 3: IMAGINE SUCCESS

PART 4: CREATE OPTIONS

PART 5: EVALUATE BARRIERS TO SUCCESS

PART 6: CHOOSE THE FUTURE

Chapter Topics

The Challenge

CHAPTER 5

DEFINE THE CHALLENGE
Solve the right problem.

Defining the challenge is step one. Addressing the challenge is step two.

You may have a product that could open a new market for the company. A strong competitor may have come into your market. Or perhaps you are concerned the organization is drifting, and you want to revitalize its value proposition. When your organization has a compelling opportunity or is threatened by new developments, start by making sure you understand the challenge—the problem you are trying to solve.

The Create the Future process takes you and your leadership team through three steps as preparation for finding the best response to the challenge:

- Define the challenge.
- Describe success.
- Establish goals.

This chapter begins your goals setting work by defining the challenge facing the organization.

The chapter's topic is:

The Challenge
Starting with why there is an opportunity or threat, define the challenge in a form that leads to a description of success and implementable goals.

This chapter gives you the tools for defining the challenge and includes an exercise in which the Team hears your challenge description, brings its insights into the discussion, and prepares a Challenge Statement.

As the company's leader, clearly defining the challenge facing the company is your responsibility. Expressing the challenge in a way that motivates others to address it is also your responsibility. This chapter's exercise engages the Team to help you define the challenge. Profiling success and establishing measurable goals are the work of Chapter 6, "Success, Goals, and Values."

If you had one hour to save the world, how would you spend that hour? Albert Einstein is credited with saying, "I would spend 55 minutes defining the problem and five minutes solving it."

When a problem confronts us, we often look for ways to mitigate the symptoms rather than address the underlying forces that create the problem. When faced with a difficult challenge, slow down. Make sure you fully understand the challenge before attempting to solve it.

As the VP of Marketing and Sales, you could say, "Sales of our lead product are declining. What can we do to get the sales force to sell more?" The sales force could be a problem, but it may not be the primary problem. A better approach is to discover the drivers of declining sales and compose a response directly addressing the primary reasons sales are declining.

You may believe you have a complete and accurate understanding of the company's challenge and don't need help defining it. Even when you believe you understand the problem, you will benefit from the Team's review and comments. A richer and perhaps different understanding of the problem will emerge.

You will get better results if you engage the Team to define the problem before asking them to solve it. The Team will have evaluated both the symptoms and the underlying drivers of the opportunity or threat. They will better understand the issues and will develop a commitment to solving the problem.

As preparation for beginning the CTF work, you described the challenge you want the Team's help addressing (Exercise 3-2, "The Problem—The

---

Engage the Team to define the problem before asking them to solve it.

Leader's Statement"). Exercise 5-1, "The Challenge," asks the Team to describe the company's opportunity or threat. The result is a Challenge Statement, which becomes the basis for defining success and establishing goals.

The exercise has two barriers you must manage:

- There may not be a simple answer.
- The Team may not believe you want to hear the answer.

Do NOT begin the exercise by distributing a written copy of *The Problem— The Leader's Statement*. If the Team believes there is already an "official answer" to the question, their contributions will be superficial, at best.

Your message to the Team must be:

- Here is what we know.
- Here are initial thoughts on the problem.
- Your help is essential for making sure we address the right challenge.

Be clear that you are open to each member's views and contributions. Use the ask, discover, and learn steps to go beyond your initial concept of the opportunity or threat.

You can ask for the Team's help with opening statements such as:

> We have three new products ready to launch. We cannot launch all three. Which should we launch first?
>
> OR
>
> Our customers are moving away from using our products and products like ours. What should we do?

Defining the first challenge may include characterizing the company's limitations on launching a new product. There may not be a simple description of the second challenge. Forces creating the threat may not be clearly visible, and several inquiry steps may be needed.

"We don't know what is happening!" is a possible conclusion. Identifying the underlying reasons sales are declining and expressing those reasons in a form that is a solvable problem may require a cycle of inquiry and discovery. Outlining a discovery process to gather additional information or doing a small experiment could be this exercise's "work product," at least for the first round.

If the conclusion of the meeting is to pause and do research outside the Team meeting, be clear that "solving the problem" is not the goal. A clear and actionable definition of the challenge is the goal. With additional information in hand, you will reconvene the meeting.

What's the Problem?

What's the Problem?

Us — **What we know** — **Them**

Us:
- Advertising + marketing out of date
- Poor sales incentives
- Out of date products
- Old technology
- Poor service

What we know:
- Declining Sales

Them:
- Changing customer preferences
- Low price competitors
- Who is best customer?
- What does customer want to buy

→ Problem Statement

At the conclusion of the exercise, if you and the Team believe you defined the Challenge with sufficient clarity and scope to develop an actionable go-forward plan, the concluding Challenge Statement will be the starting point for defining "success" in Chapter 6, "Success, Goals, and Values."

Exercise 5-1
The Challenge

The Team defines the challenge facing the organization in this exercise. Company leaders begin by sharing their understanding of the opportunity or threat. The Team evaluates the forces underlying the challenge, bringing their knowledge, insights, and accessible resources into the discussion. The Team then prepares a Challenge Statement.

Exercise Steps

- Leaders who initiated the CTF work start the exercise by sharing their understanding of the opportunity or threat.
- Ask the Team to discuss the challenge. Is there a different way to describe it or understand it? What forces are creating it? Why is this an opportunity or threat?
- Ask if the Team has enough information to define the challenge. If not, what is needed, and what can you do to get it?
- If the Team believes it can define the challenge, ask for a description of the opportunity or threat.

Exercise Work Product

- Challenge Statement defining the opportunity or threat facing the company and driving the CTF work

The whiteboard postings go in the Team Meeting Notes section of the Decision Book. A photograph of the whiteboard may be sufficient to capture the Team's work, or a modest elaboration of the notes may be needed to preserve the ideas and conclusions. Create a stand-alone version of the Challenge Statement to include with the Meeting Notes and in the Challenges sections of the Decision Book and the Decision Package.

KEY TAKEAWAYS

1. Defining the challenge is the first step to finding a solution.
2. Engage the Team to define the problem before asking them to solve it.
3. As the company's leader, clearly defining the challenge facing the company is your responsibility. Expressing the challenge in a way that motivates others to address it is also your responsibility.
4. Be clear to the Team that you are open to their views and contributions.

PART 1: PREPARE THE COMPANY AND YOURSELF

PART 2: DEFINE THE CHALLENGE

PART 3: IMAGINE SUCCESS

PART 4: CREATE OPTIONS

PART 5: EVALUATE BARRIERS TO SUCCESS

PART 6: CHOOSE THE FUTURE

Chapter Topics

Success Is a Choice

Success—Aspiration and Strategy

Success as an Expression of Values

Goals—Operational Targets

CHAPTER 6

SUCCESS, GOALS, AND VALUES
What success looks like.

You have defined the Challenge. What will success look like if you exploit the opportunity or counter the threat?

Success can be an aspirational statement and can be quantified operational goals. Success is also a choice. In this chapter, I develop the concept of success and profile three exercises characterizing and quantifying success for your organization.

The chapter topics are:

Success Is a Choice
Both the concept of success and the goals you establish for measuring success are choices you make.

Success—Aspiration and Strategy
Success is an aspiration and can be a strategy statement—how you will compete to win.

Success as an Expression of Values
Values may be expressed by the organization's strategy and operations. If so, you must develop guidelines for considering these values when a response to the Challenge is selected.

Goals—Operational Targets
Goals are performance targets for achieving success.

SUCCESS IS A CHOICE

Legendary American basketball coach Rick Pitino wrote a book titled *Success Is a Choice*. Pitino shared his experience working with talented young players who transformed themselves into top performers and championship teams. The transformational moment was when they chose to be successful. They stopped being "a talented basketball player" and decided to become a "champion."

Success could be staying in your comfort zone and doing what you are already doing, or success could be a hard-to-achieve stretch goal. Success is a choice for your organization, just as it is for you as an individual.

Some leaders will imagine several go-forward options for the company and select one of the options. That option becomes "the plan." In effect, they define success as the consequence of the path they choose rather than defining success as a goal to be achieved and then finding the best path to reach that level of success.

In Chapter 8, "Choices for the Future," you will imagine options for making the company "successful." These options, the Choices, will be analyzed in the following chapters, and then you will select the preferred path forward Choice. Best practice is to start with a clear concept of success. Before imagining different ways to address the challenge before you, settle on a concept of what success would look like.

We profile Success in three categories: Goals, Risk Preferences, and Values. You may include others. With success defined, then find the path forward that best matches your goals, risk preference, and values. Without a concept of success, all plans will be successful.

Think about success in two steps:

- The character of success—the aspiration, the strategy, and the values
- The measurement of success—the goals

Success is a choice.

Without a concept of success, all plans will be successful.

Character gets at what success will be like. You characterize the quality of what you hope to achieve and your strategy for achieving success. Will you grow, sell, launch, coast, harvest, or what? Then quantify the level of success by setting "goals." How much will revenues grow? When will the new product be launched? You must choose both the character of success and the level of success.

Nothing is simple. Considering the dilemma other leaders faced when defining success will broaden your thinking about success for your organization and for yourself. From the following examples, I hope you see that leaders in each of these situations have a range of options for defining success. For them and you, success is a choice.

- *You have a new product to bring to market. You will need outside financing for marketing and sales development. You must establish goals for the product that capture its value but do not put the company at risk.*

- *The division you run is seen as a cash cow. The corporation wants to limit costs, but the division's products must stay competitive to maintain their market position. You must define success for the operational and investment initiatives you will propose.*

- *You are the executive director of a regional transitional housing and shelter provider. Foundation and donor support are essential. Your funders are urging you to operate more cost effectively. You must include program and operational goals in your recommendations to the board.*

- *The company is financially stable in a market with modest growth opportunities. The company has not made acquisitions or invested in new product development. You are the new CEO, and family owners want to raise the company's value for a possible sale. How will you define success in the proposal you will make for raising the company's value?*

▸ *The testing instrument your company sells has been the lower-cost alternative in the market. Your higher-quality and higher-cost competitor has introduced a testing service as an alternative to selling the instrument. Sales of instruments core to your business are flat, and you hear that buying the testing service is an option your customers are considering. Your board asked how they should judge the company's performance and your performance over the next two to three years.*

▸ *Your company provides a range of security services, from building security to security details. You are considering purchasing a company that owns and operates prisons. If you make the acquisition, what would success look like from a financial and strategic perspective? What values will the prison operations express, and how will the company project the values to the public?*

Choose Success before Founding the Company

Two faculty members at MIT asked me to join them and found a company exploiting technology they developed for dramatically faster DNA sequencing. At the time, DNA sequencing was a high-skill, lengthy process, and their approach had lots of promise. I talked with them over several weeks about the business opportunity and my becoming CEO of the company. I identified initial funding for the company. A barrier emerged that we could not get past. One of the founders believed that funding for the company would mostly be more funding for his lab.

He was not, in the end, interested in founding a company to make and sell products. He did not want to leave his lab and did not understand that working in the lab and founding a company are two different activities. Both are valid, but they are different. Getting clarity about our individual goals for the company saved the three of us from what could have been a long, frustrating attempt to create a company with founders having very different expectations for success.

SUCCESS—ASPIRATION AND STRATEGY

Every morning, the sun is shining, or rain pelts your windows. That day, you will have opportunities, and you will face threats. You can approach each day with joy and determination, or you can approach each day with a sense of resignation as you deal with one problem after another. Stay in bed if your plan for the day is to take the second approach.

Effective leaders have a vision of success—rain or shine. They approach each opportunity and threat as a time to learn, innovate, and succeed. The impactful leader changes uncertainty into hope and possibility.

> *During the height of the COVID-19 pandemic of 2020–2021, air travel collapsed. Ed Bastian, CEO of Delta Airlines, described his job as a unique opportunity.*
>
> *"I look at this moment as an opportunity and not a burden. I am privileged to be the leader of Delta as we find our way through the challenges COVID presents us."*

Before designing your organization's one-year, two-year, or five-year plan, you need a concept of success. For example, is success selling the company for the highest possible price with a portion of the payment contingent on future performance? Or is success selling the company for cash on closing? You have a great new product to introduce. Do you want to build market share or generate free cash flow to pay off loans? Is success saving the company from bankruptcy or selling the company for whatever you can get?

You may have a concept of success and are doubtful the Team can add value to your thinking. Stay open to different ways to think about success. Challenge your leadership team, the CTF Team, and yourself to imagine success in different ways. Think broadly and creatively and learn from their perspectives. Ask what the company will have accomplished if it is successful over the next one, three, or five years—the relevant time horizon. What are you trying to accomplish? Engaging the Team will expand the conversation about success and establish shared expectations for success.

The impactful leader changes uncertainty into hope and possibility.

Before designing your organization's one-year, two-year, or five- year plan, you need a concept of success.

Divide the definition of success into two parts:

- **Success Statement:** For example, "We will sell this company in three years."

- **Operational Goals Statement:** For example, "We will grow EBITDA from $3 million to $6 million, which will raise the sale price multiple on EBITDA from 6 to 8 and then sell the company for $40 million or more."

Differentiating between Success and Operational Goals encourages you to express your complete concept of success. Exercise 6-1 focuses on success as an aspiration and strategy. Exercise 6-2 gives you and the organization's other leaders a forum to include social mission values in the aspirational and operational goals. Exercise 6-3 defines the quantitative and operational levels of success.

Exercises 6-1 and 6-2 develop a Success Statement that describes what the company will accomplish. The statement can include the following:

- Aspiration
- Strategy
- Permission
- Constraint

Aspiration is what the organization will accomplish. "We will expand our property, casualty, and liability insurance product lines to recreational vehicles and boats." Strategy is how you will compete. "We will be a low-cost insurer for low-risk customers." The Success Statement also sets boundaries on what the organization will and will not do to achieve its strategic and operational goals.

Finding the best strategy and business model optimized for the company where it is today and where it hopes to go tomorrow is beyond the scope of this book. (See Chapter 7 for more on strategy and the business model in the CTF context.) If changing the company's business strategy or business model is part of the plan, include executing the new strategy as part of the definition of success. Moving from a commodity player competing on price to a specialty producer competing on differentiated products and services is hard to do. If that is the success goal, spell it out.

All organizations have financial, manpower, time, capacity, intellectual property (IP), leadership, and other limitations to achieving success. Where the company will operate within these resource constraints should be specified in the Success Statement. If securing outside financing might be needed to pay for a new initiative, the Success Statement should specify whether raising new equity or debt is permitted.

If getting the Team's views on the concept of success and building a consensus on its definition is valuable, take the Team through these exercises and the following operational goals exercise. The company leadership must be clear that they are open to hearing Team members' views. Minimize official and leadership statements about what success should be.

Success

These exercises create a Success Statement. You may want to combine the Challenge Statement from Exercise 5-1, "The Challenge," and the Success Statement into a simplified leadership message. Usually, a leadership message is needed that captures both the problem and the vision of success. The combined message is the Vision Statement. The Vision Statement expresses the intent of company leadership and is also a path-forward vision for employees and others connected with the company and possibly its customers and suppliers.

Vision Statements could be, We will . . .

- ▸ Introduce the new screening test to the market and reduce colon cancer.
- ▸ Stop the decline of this company and preserve as much value as possible for the shareholders.
- ▸ Bring our low-cost construction technology to areas with major housing shortages.

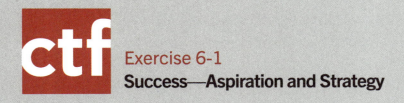

Exercise 6-1
Success—Aspiration and Strategy

In this exercise, the Team describes success as an aspiration and possibly a strategy. The Team describes success qualitatively and identifies permissions for and restraints on achieving success. Success is combined with the Challenge to create a Vision Statement.

Exercise Steps

- Post a description or distribute a copy of the Challenge Statement. Ask the organization's leader to describe a successful outcome for the organization's response to the opportunity or threat.
- Ask the Team what they believe success could look like.
- If changes to the company's strategy (how it competes) or its business model (how it makes a profit) are planned, ask for a description of the new strategy/business model.
- Ask what *constraints* should be placed on achieving success. Ask what *permissions* should be given.
- Ask how much or how little the constraints or permissions should apply. Use a scale such as—Always Control, Control If . . . , Come Back for Approval.
- Ask for comments on the posted descriptions of success.
- Ask for a description of success supported by most Team members. This becomes the Success Statement.
- Ask for a brief description of the Challenge and Success combined into an aspirational Vision Statement.

Exercise Work Products

- Success Statement qualitatively describing success and the permissions and constraints on what the organization can and cannot do to achieve success.
- A Vision Statement describing the challenge and profiling a vision of success.

SUCCESS AS AN EXPRESSION OF VALUES

Leaders want their organization to express values important to them. These values influence how the organization conducts its business and how it operates internally. All companies and organizations have "values." Maximizing shareholder value is a "values statement." Risk tolerance is a values statement.

The Success Statement and the Goals Statement should reflect or at least not conflict with the values of the company's leaders. In some cases, company owners will have social, environmental, or philanthropic causes they want the company to support or express through its operations. Ben & Jerry's, the iconic ice cream brand, is a classic example of a values-driven company. The founders were far ahead of their time, driving the company to recycle and protect the environment. When they sold the company to Unilever, one of the conditions of the sale was that Ben & Jerry's continue as a separate subsidiary in the United States, expressing "progressive" values, such as being "committed to honoring the rights of all people to live with liberty, security, self-esteem, and freedom of expression and protest."

Owners like Ben and Jerry want their values considered when making important decisions. If supporting these values limits other "performance" levels, that is an acceptable trade-off for them. If the organization is a non-profit, educational institution, or government agency, nonfinancial values can be central to its mission and its aspirational Success Statement.

Most CTF exercises draw out the Team's views so the Decision Makers will benefit from hearing their input and perspective. This exercise gives deference to the Decider's views. The Values Statement created by the exercise should reflect the views of the Decision Makers.

If the organization's Decision Makers need guidance on how to consider the organization's values when selecting the preferred Future Choice, take the Team through Exercise 6-2, "Success as an Expression of Values." This exercise may identify social, economic, environmental, equity, and other values leaders want the organization to express by what it does and how it operates. Child labor practices and the education of future engineers could be examples. Preserving distributable income could be a values statement for a family owned business.

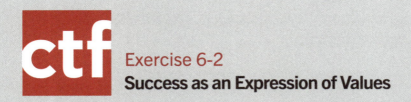

Exercise 6-2
Success as an Expression of Values

This exercise identifies values company leaders and owners will consider when selecting the preferred Future Choice. The organization's leadership also characterizes the degree to which these values will limit the Future Choice selection.

Exercise Steps

- Ask Decision Makers on the Team to identify values they believe should be considered when evaluating options for responding to the organization's opportunity or threat.
- Ask other Team members what values they suggest.
- Ask which values are relevant to potential responses to the organization's Challenge and are important enough to be included in the Success Statement. Ask why the Deciders should include these values.
- Ask how these values should be applied when selecting the Future Choice. Use a scale such as complete control, strong influence, or preference when possible.
- Ask for a Values Statement supported by most Decision Makers. Include a description of the values to be expressed and the degree of control these values will have when the Future Choice is selected and implemented.
- Incorporate the Values Statement into a revised Success Statement.

Exercise Work Products

- A Values Statement describing values to be considered when the preferred Future Choice is selected.
- Addition of the Values Statement to the Success Statement and the Vision Statement.

Values can be central to the organization's aspirational Success Statement.

GOALS—OPERATIONAL TARGETS

You profiled Success. The Team next establishes operational goals that define when you have achieved success, Exercise 6-3, "Goals—Operational Targets."

Operational goals are usually quantified performance targets such as revenue growth, a higher operating margin, or the value of new equity financing. You also need to consider the time for achieving the operational goal and where you want to be on the degree of difficulty scale.

Usually, the qualitative concept of success can be satisfied by different quantitative performance levels. Successfully growing revenues could be defined as reaching 3%, 8%, or 15%. The time frame for achieving the specified level of performance could be three months, six months, or two years.

Specifying an expected performance level is also specifying where you will be on the degree-of-difficulty scale. The more challenging the goal, the greater the risk of not reaching the goal. Is failure an acceptable risk? Setting operational, qualitative goals requires choosing where to set the standard of success on the degree-of-difficulty range and the risk/reward scale.

Are you continuing gradual growth or challenging your sales and production capabilities? Is this initiative an "experiment," or does the organization's future depend on the initiative's success? You must weigh the importance of achieving success as established by these operational goals against the value of what you will learn even if the initiative is not successful. Was the risk of failure worth the investment of time and resources?

Keep it simple. Make the goal easy to understand and translate into an implementation plan. A complex set of goals will dilute the message of focusing everyone's efforts on achieving an important and clearly understood objective.

Operational Goal

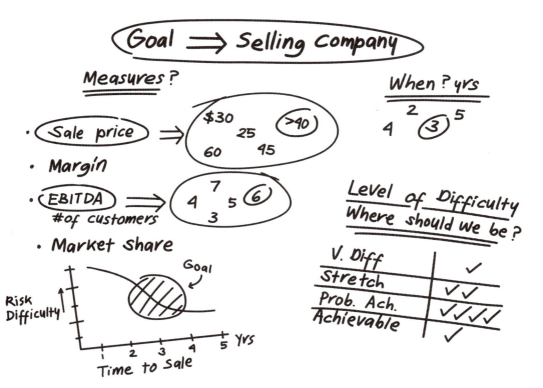

After composing the Success Statement, you will usually quantify success expectations and specify operational targets but not always. For example, Colon Detect was a start-up with no revenue founded by two cancer researchers. Their Vision Statement was, "We want to introduce our new screening test to the market and reduce avoidable colon cancer." They used the CTF exercises to identify a viable business model that could bring the new test to the market. They did not specify revenue or profitability goals at this stage of their work to create the company.

Keep it simple. Make the goal easy to understand and translate into an implementation plan.

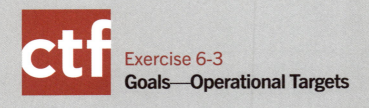

Exercise 6-3
Goals—Operational Targets

This exercise creates quantitative-operational goals as execution targets within the framework established by the Success Statement.

Exercise Steps

- Post or distribute a copy of the Success Statement.
- Ask how to measure success—what to measure and not the level of success.
- Ask for a consensus on what single performance measure or a small number of measures should be used to determine success.
- Ask what level of performance will define "success."
- Ask what time will be allowed for achieving the performance goals.
- Ask the Team to characterize different combinations of performance level and elapsed time as achievable, probably achievable, stretch goals, or very difficult to achieve. These comments characterize the possible operational goals by their degree of difficulty.
- Ask for a consensus operational goal with a level of performance and a time for achieving that level of performance acceptable to most Team members.
- Write a consensus Operational Goals Statement.

Exercise Work Product

- Operational Goals Statement including the level of performance and the time for achieving success.

Another company, Can Do Trucking, was a stable, family-owned business with $100 million of revenue. Stability and income for the family were the definition of success, over the long run. The CEO's goal was to "modestly" increase operating margins and gradually grow revenue while maintaining a strong financial position. The CEO asked the Team to help quantify "modest performance improvements" while keeping a strong balance sheet.

Photographs of the Team's whiteboard notes may be sufficient to capture the Team's work on the Success and Goals exercises. Or a modest elaboration of the notes may be needed to preserve the ideas and conclusions. File the notes in the Team Meeting Notes section of the Decision Book. File copies of the Success Statement, the Vision Statement, and the Operational Goals Statement in the Notes and Goals sections of the Decision Book as stand-alone documents.

KEY TAKEAWAYS

1. Before designing your organization's one-year, two-year, or five-year plan, you need a concept of success.
2. The impactful leader changes uncertainty into hope and possibility.
3. Success is a choice.
4. Without a concept of success, all plans will be successful.
5. Keep it simple. Make the goal easy to understand and translate into an implementation plan.

PART 1: PREPARE THE COMPANY AND YOURSELF

PART 2: DEFINE THE CHALLENGE

PART 3: IMAGINE SUCCESS

PART 4: CREATE OPTIONS

PART 5: EVALUATE BARRIERS TO SUCCESS

PART 6: CHOOSE THE FUTURE

Chapter Topics

Categories of Future Choices

Strategy and Business Model
—Important, but a Separate Discussion

CHAPTER 7

PATHS TO SUCCESS
Different ways to solve the problem.

You have a vision of success. Now engage the Team's creative powers to identify different ways to reach the success goals.

This chapter's topics are:

Categories of Future Choices
Identify categories of initiatives that can address the challenge.

Strategy and Business Model—Important, but a Separate Discussion
Developing a business strategy and business model appropriate to your company where it is today is important but is a separate topic that CTF does not directly address.

Start the process for finding the go-forward Future Choice that will achieve your success goals by imagining categories of initiatives you could pursue. This chapter includes an exercise identifying categories of Future Choices that become the framework for the ideation work in Chapter 8, "Choices for the Future." I also distinguish between CTF's decision-making-process work and the related work of designing a business strategy specific to your company.

CATEGORIES OF FUTURE CHOICES
Before proposing specific initiatives you could pursue to take advantage of the opportunity or counter the threat, ask a broader question: What categories of options do you have for achieving success and reaching your goals? Imagine categories of initiatives before trying to define the best response. Identifying several paths you might pursue to achieve the goals will expand your thinking about how to achieve success.

The Team will be more creative if it first identifies categories of options for solving the problem rather than jumping to a specific solution for the problem.

The Team will be more creative if it first identifies categories of options for solving the problem rather than jumping to a specific solution for the problem. In other words, before asking the Team to generate individual ideas for higher profitability, raising capital, or cutting costs, identify different clusters, paths, or categories of ways to accomplish these goals.

Here is an example of a solution very different from first appearances. The owner of an office building in New York received complaints from tenants about slow elevator service. Some even threatened not to renew their lease because of it. The building owner asked the elevator management company to find a way to make the elevators run faster. While the riders did not like waiting, they also did not like the elevator dropping quickly. There was no way to run the elevators faster.

The building owner expressed his frustration at a monthly staff meeting. A new hire in the sales office suggested a different way to think about the slow elevators. As an experiment, they installed mirrors on the walls around the elevators. People waiting for the elevator looked at themselves and others in the mirrors and did not notice how long they waited for the elevator. Complaints about slow elevator service stopped.

The building owner initially believed his problem was a slow elevator. After stepping back and considering "the problem" more carefully, he explored different categories of solutions. One category was changing the elevator's operations. Another category was engaging with the tenants while they waited for the elevator. Better understanding the problem, clarifying success, and exploring different categories of solutions solved the tenant complaint problem. (Example taken from *Turning Learning Right Side Up: Putting Education Back on Track* by Dr. Russell Ackoff and Daniel Greenberg.)

Consider the company that wants to grow revenues. The Team Leader or facilitator will pose a question to the Team such as, "Over the next three years, the goal we have established for the company is to grow annual revenue each year by 8 percent or greater on average. How can we achieve that goal?"

Before asking the Team, "How do we grow revenue?" ask the broader question, "What are different ways we could grow revenues?" Ask what categories of options the Team can imagine for growing revenues.

The categories of possible revenue growth could be:

- Increase market share with current customers
- Introduce new products
- Expand into new categories of customers
- Raise prices
- Develop new products
- Acquire a company or product line

These categories of possible solutions become the structure within which you will ask for lots of ideas for "how to grow revenues." Identifying Categories of Future Choices before beginning the creative "all ideas are good ideas" work will put more, and perhaps better, options on the whiteboard. These options will also encourage company leaders to be clear about what they want to achieve and what options they will not consider.

One way to encourage a range of execution proposals is to begin with "little change" and go by steps to "moonshot" options. These Categories of Future Choices will get your thinking started.

- *Little change*—mostly maintain current operations
- *Modest changes/initiatives*—easily achievable initiatives and changes
- *Stretch initiatives*—achievable initiatives/changes challenging the organization
- *Moonshot initiatives*—initiatives beyond what is clearly achievable with important benefits if successful

You may not want to take a moonshot risk, and you may want more than "business as usual." But putting those options on the table loosens constraints on the Team's thinking.

Categories of Future Choices—Examples

These companies used the categories of options approach.

Digital Wellness Software—Product Distribution

A digital wellness software company leader shared with me their Future Choices Categories. These are product launch distribution options changed slightly to keep confidentiality.

The product was a personalized high-tech and high-touch digital wellness delivery platform. The individual consumer is the ultimate buyer. Before formulating a launch plan, they identified categories of distribution channels for the product. The first category split is selling directly to consumers or selling to businesses (distributors) who would sell the product to consumers. The distribution channels included:

COMPANY TO BUSINESS TO CONSUMER
- Physician practices
- Health and fitness clubs
- Health insurance companies
- Hospital and medical center

COMPANY TO CONSUMER
- Direct sales to consumers through social media
- Direct sales to consumers through pharmacies

By first identifying possible distribution channels, they created a more-comprehensive range of launch options and better understood the advantages and disadvantages of each category of launch options.

Categories of Future Choices

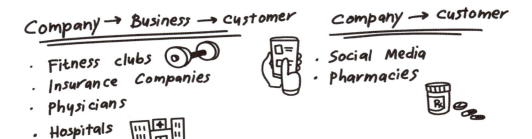

Printing Company Products

A printing company owner took his Team through CTF exercises to find new markets for their services. Whiteboard postings for new product ideas included business cards, advertising mailers, and company brochures. The printing company could make those products, but they did not have a competitive advantage making or marketing them for their broad range of potential customers.

The facilitator asked the Team to step back and identify categories of products or services where the printing company might have a competitive advantage. Team members suggested product categories that might make them the preferred supplier as well as categories of specialized customers. Finding categories of opportunities where they might be able to distinguish themselves from their competitors was the goal.

Trynka Shineman grew Vista Print to over $1 billion in revenues by focusing on products for microbusinesses with one to five employees.

Exercise 7-1, "Categories of Future Choices," asks the Team to identify categories of options for achieving Success and reaching the Goal. Take the Team through this exercise before asking them to propose specific plans and initiatives for achieving the success goals.

Exercise 7-1
Categories of Future Choices

This exercise identifies categories of options for achieving Success and reaching the organization's Goals. These categories should apply to this organization but not be judged as to whether they are the best approach for reaching the goal. The Team may also identify categories of options to be excluded.

Exercise Steps

- Ask the Team what categories of options and initiatives might achieve the organization's success goals. Identifying specific initiatives for reaching the goal is not the objective.
- Ask if there are categories of initiatives to include, from little change to "moonshot."
- Of the categories listed, ask if subcategories with significant potential should be broken out separately.
- Consolidate the listed categories into manageable categories to be used as the structure for the "all ideas are good ideas" work.
- Ask if there are categories of initiatives that should not be considered.

Exercise Work Products

- Categories of Future Choices for achieving the company's goals
- No-Go Categories—initiatives not to be considered

A photo or modestly elaborated record of the Team's whiteboard notes will go in the Team Meeting Notes section of the Decision Book. File stand-alone versions of the Categories of Future Choices and the list of No-Go Categories in the Meeting Notes section and the Choices for the Future section of the Book.

The Categories of Future Choices will be the framework for the Future Choices work of Chapter 8.

STRATEGY AND BUSINESS MODEL
—IMPORTANT, BUT A SEPARATE DISCUSSION

Your business's long-term success requires a smart strategy and a financially viable business model. Successfully competing means the company has a successful strategy. Making a profit means the company has a viable business model.

Strategy
Application of resources available to create a competitive advantage while delivering value to the customer

Business Model
Combination of creating and selling products that deliver value to the customer while being financially rewarding to the company and its owners

When McDonald's was a small company, it sold hamburgers and fries. McDonald's did not sell donuts or salads or pizza. It sold hamburgers and fries. The company built thousands of stores selling hamburgers and fries. Not until McDonald's had a national and international chain of outlets did it look for other products to sell in its franchise outlets.

> MCDONALD'S STRATEGY WAS:
>
> McDonald's will be a branded chain of fast-food retailers primarily selling hamburgers and fries at competitive prices. McDonald's products will be the same at every outlet and be consistently high quality. Growth and brand awareness are the goals.

> MCDONALD'S BUSINESS MODEL WAS:
>
> McDonald's will be a franchise business with standardized supplies, processes, procedures, branding, and outlet design. Local franchise owners will purchase their franchise to be located at an approved site, built to McDonald's specifications, and will sell only McDonald's products at approved prices.

Offering one product was the growth strategy. Offering complementary products was the "raise revenues per store" strategy after a successful one-product strategy to build market share.

Founders of early stage companies are often excited by many potential applications of their technology or service. Pursuing multiple product lines in several business sectors is a losing strategy. Young companies must focus on providing one product or service better than anyone else. The business goal is to win paying customers, build revenues, and make a "profit."

Successful strategies for established companies in mature markets are quite different from the strategies of high-growth companies. McDonald's strategy today probably includes reducing revenue and EBITDA volatility, ensuring supply chain security, and protecting the brand. The business model includes reducing costs and growing revenue per outlet.

Let me put these topics in the CTF context. CTF is an Ask, Discover, Learn, and Decide approach for addressing any complex problem, including choosing your competitive strategy or business model. You can use CTF exercises to evaluate the strategy and business plan options you develop. You will more fully understand their implications before choosing the best strategy for your company, given its resources and where it is today in its competitive environment. This book does not develop strategy and business-model concepts and how they might apply to your company where it is today. Those concepts are beyond the scope of this book.

In the end, you will choose the company's path forward drawing on your experience, considering the Team's advice, and applying your judgment. As part of that decision, be explicit about the strategy you are pursuing and the business model you will implement—write them out. The Future Choices you evaluate and the final Choice you select as the path forward for the

---

Successfully competing means the company has a successful strategy. Making a profit means the company has a viable business model.

company should express the strategy and the business model you are currently pursuing or intend to implement.

Strategy and Business Model—Additional Resources
If developing a competitive strategy and business model is an important consideration when choosing the path forward for the company, these resources can be helpful. They cover the basics and have references to other sources.

- *Strategy* by Harvard Business School Press
- *Strategic Planning* by John H. Dobbs and John F. Dobbs
- *Competitive Strategy* by Michael Porter
- *Understanding Michael Porter* by Joan Magretta
- *Developing Business Strategies* by David Aaker
- *Gaining and Sustaining Competitive Advantage* by Jay Barney

---

KEY TAKEAWAYS

1. Before proposing specific initiatives your organization could pursue, ask what categories of options you have for achieving success and reaching your goals.
2. Successfully competing means the company has a successful strategy. Making a profit means the company has a viable business model.
3. The Future Choices you evaluate and the final Choice you select as the path forward for the company should express the strategy and the business model you are currently pursuing or intend to implement.

PART 1: PREPARE THE COMPANY AND YOURSELF

PART 2: DEFINE THE CHALLENGE

PART 3: IMAGINE SUCCESS

PART 4: CREATE OPTIONS

PART 5: EVALUATE BARRIERS TO SUCCESS

PART 6: CHOOSE THE FUTURE

Chapter Topics

All Ideas Are Good Ideas

Selecting Choices for the Future

Benefits of the Future Choices

CHAPTER 8

CHOICES FOR THE FUTURE
Create options for the path to success.

Future thinking—where the company could go—is this chapter's focus.

Creating ideas, including crazy ideas, for exploiting the opportunity or addressing the threat is where this work begins.

Even if you believe you know the best way to address the company's challenge, pause and allow for the possibility that other options are worth considering.

The Choices for the Future work in this chapter begins with generating lots of ideas and ends with profiling the benefits of the Choices created.

The chapter topics are:

All Ideas Are Good Ideas
"All ideas are good ideas" is the creative call to action for identifying many possible options for achieving the company's goals.

Selecting Choices for the Future
You distill many Choices for the Future options into a small number of Choices for the Future to be considered in more depth.

Benefits of the Future Choices
The Team profiles the Future Choices by their benefits to the company.

ALL IDEAS ARE GOOD IDEAS
Create the Future combines "all ideas are good ideas" creativity with disciplined reality. The exercises in this chapter create options for addressing the challenge facing your organization. The reality check comes with Chapter 9's examination of the execution barriers to realizing the benefits of the Future Choices.

The Team created a framework for the "all ideas" work in Chapters 6 and 7 by developing the following:

- Success and Operational Goals Statements
- Categories of Future Choices

The Categories of Future Choices identified different categories of ways your organization could address the opportunity or threat you face. The "All Ideas Are Good Ideas" exercise, described in this chapter, puts options on the whiteboard for achieving the company's goals in these categories. The work product will be an unranked list of possible initiatives to consider.

In Chapter 7, a digital wellness company identified categories of possible distribution channels for their new products. Some channels sold directly to consumers, and others went through resellers like doctor's offices. These categories of channels become the framework for the "all ideas" work, imagining specific product distribution ideas—lots of ideas. The following illustration captures that company's possible distribution options within the Choices Categories.

"All Ideas Are Good Ideas"—Digital Product Launch

Before describing the "All Ideas Are Good Ideas" exercise, I want to get you in an "all ideas are good ideas" frame of mind, which is not the normal mind frame for most of us. If you have not already done so, read the CTF Thinking way of problem-solving and creative brainstorming in Chapter 1. Be sure everyone is on board with listening to other points of view and "what is said in the room stays in the room." Encourage unbounded and unconventional "all ideas are good ideas" thinking.

Let's get started with the CTF exercises that guide you to imagining different ways you could achieve the Success you profiled. Run through Exercise 8-1, "All Ideas Are Good Ideas," by starting with the possible solutions categories, and let the ideas flow. The reality work comes later. This exercise creates options for addressing the Challenge facing the company and achieving its Goals. The objective is to create ideas and options with little restraint on practicality. Ask the Team to offer lots of ideas. Don't ask for "great ideas." Start with lots of ideas, and then find the great ideas on the whiteboard.

"All Ideas Are Good Ideas" is a "Team exercise." Even if the "Team" is you by yourself or just two of you creating a new initiative, you can use the steps in this exercise as your step-by-step guideline for getting options on the whiteboard with limited conventional-thinking boundaries.

When you and your CTF Team are ready, put on your Mardi Gras beads, tropical shirts, or whatever else might make this a creative moment.

Don't ask for "great ideas." Start with lots of ideas, and then find the great ideas on the whiteboard.

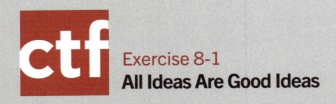

Exercise 8-1
All Ideas Are Good Ideas

This exercise creates many ideas for addressing the Challenge facing your organization. With the *Categories of Future Choices* as a framework, imagine a wide range of options for addressing the Challenge. Encourage unconventional thinking. In this exercise, all ideas are good ideas.

Exercise Steps

- Start with the Goals Statement and the Categories of Future Choices as the framework for imagining initiatives the company could pursue.
- Ask the Team for possible initiatives that could achieve the goals within each category of possible solutions.
- From the options suggested, look for themes and different ways to solve the problem that suggest other alternatives.
- Identify no more than twelve options for further consideration.
- Identify options or categories of options that are not to be considered (the No-Go Options).

Exercise Work Products

- Long List of Future Choices for achieving the organization's goals
- No-Go Options not to be considered further

If the "All Ideas Are Good Ideas" exercise creates many ideas, they are probably in the following four categories:

- Worth serious consideration
- Might achieve goals but not clear they can be implemented
- Cannot achieve goals (although it may be a good tactical idea for the company staff to consider)
- No-Go options

Select twelve or fewer unique Future Choices worth consideration and further development. Do not rank or judge which is best—you will whittle them down in Exercise 8-2. However, if the Long List of Future Choices is six or fewer Future Choices and they are good options, declare success and don't do Exercise 8-2. In this case, the Long List becomes the Choices for the Future that will be carried through the analysis and selection steps.

A photo of the whiteboard or a modestly elaborated record of the Team's whiteboard notes will go in the Team Meeting Notes section of the Decision Book. Create cleaned-up and stand-alone versions of the Long List of Future Choices (the Choices for the Future, if applicable) and the list of No-Go Options, and file those in the Meeting Notes and the Choices for the Future sections.

The "All Ideas" discussion may have revealed No-Go options that had not surfaced earlier. ("Why don't we just sell the company?" may have been posted on the board. "We are not selling the company!" could have been your response or a major shareholder's response.) If limitations on future options emerge, record them, and update the Goals Statement in the Decision Book.

SELECTING CHOICES FOR THE FUTURE

The "All Ideas Are Good Ideas" exercise puts options on the whiteboard. Being nonjudgmental was core to the "all ideas" work. The last step of Exercise 8-1 was limiting the All Ideas list to no more than twelve Choices. Keeping more than five or six new initiatives under consideration is usually too demanding.

If more than six options remain at the end of Exercise 8-1, do Exercise 8-2, "Choices for the Future," and whittle down the list of options to a smaller number of Choices you and the Team can effectively evaluate. Move from "all ideas are good ideas" to prioritizing the Choices and selecting those worth taking through the evaluation and decision-making steps.

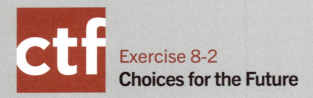

Exercise 8-2
Choices for the Future

The Long List of Future Choices included the best "all ideas are good ideas" options without careful consideration of feasibility or their capacity for achieving the organization's goals. They seemed to be reasonable Choices, but they were not carefully evaluated. Time and bandwidth limitations usually limit an in-depth analysis of possible options to six or fewer Future Choices.

In this exercise, the Team uses available information and best judgments to identify six or fewer Future Choices to be evaluated in-depth.

Exercise Steps

- ▶ Ask the Team which initiatives on the Long List of Future Choices are outside the acceptable boundaries of risk or are not likely to achieve the goals.
- ▶ Look for opportunities to consolidate options into one "big idea."
- ▶ Ask if the options are in an acceptable risk-and-reward range and if the Choices fully cover the preferred risk/reward range.
- ▶ Select six (or fewer) Choices for further evaluation.

Exercise Work Product

- ▶ Choices for the Future—six or fewer options for achieving the organization's goals

This exercise begins with the Long List of Future Choices and reduces the list to six or fewer. The goal is to limit the Choices to a manageable number to be carried through the analysis and decision-making steps. These options for addressing the threat or opportunity will not have been ranked or evaluated to be certain they are achievable. But they should be real options. You should see the Choices as sufficiently plausible to be worth further investigation.

File the exercise results in the Team Meeting Notes section of the Decision Book and include a stand-alone version of the Choices for the Future in the Meeting Notes and Choices for the Future sections.

The description of each Choice will be refined as it moves from "all ideas are good ideas" to the Long List of Future Choices and to a Choice for the Future. The All Ideas list quickly captured initial concepts. The Long List consolidated ideas and clarified core concepts. Each Choice for the Future should clearly and concisely describe a possible initiative understandable to someone who did not participate in the exercise.

When selecting the final Choices for the Future, consider the Decision Tree profile of essential Go/No-Go decisions discussed in Chapter 11. An example of a critical decision might be whether to license a technology or do an experiment to clarify feasibility. These decisions are not, in themselves, Future Choices for the company. But they will open or close off Future Choices. If relevant, reference these essential decisions in the description of Future Choices, since these decisions enable or foreclose the Future Choices under consideration.

BENEFITS OF THE FUTURE CHOICES

The Choices for the Future are options for addressing the opportunity or threat driving the CTF work. The Choices were selected in Exercise 8-1 or 8-2 by the following criteria:

- Addressing the Challenge facing the company
- Achieving the Goals
- Being potentially achievable
- If a "moonshot" is an option, failure is an acceptable outcome

Before selecting which Future Choice to pursue, Decision Makers must consider the benefits they can expect from each Choice and the risk profile of the barriers they must overcome to harvest the benefits. In Exercise 8-3, "Benefits of the Future Choices," you identify the expected benefits of each Choice for the Future. The benefits could include, for example, anticipated increases in market share, debt reduction, higher EBITDA, or a valuation step-up.

The Benefits of the Future Choices exercise creates a top-level comparative summary of the Choices displayed as a Future Choices Benefits Matrix. This information feeds into the Benefits and Barriers Matrix developed in Chapter 9 after the Team identifies the execution barriers.

Future Choices Benefits Matrix, How to Grow Revenues

Target ⇒ Grow revenue 8% annually

Choices	Benefits
Ⓐ New product	Long term revenue + profits / New customer / EBITDA?
Ⓑ Raise Sales + Marketing $	No Tech Risk / Grow revenue
Ⓒ New Customer Categories	No tech risk / No new product risk / Long term revenue + profit

Exercise 8-3
Benefits of the Future Choices

This exercise identifies the benefits of each Future Choice and displays their most important benefits in a Future Choices Benefits Matrix.

Exercise Steps

- Outline a matrix on the whiteboard with two columns: Choices and Benefits.
- List the Choices for the Future in the Choices column.
- Ask the Team to identify the Benefits of each Choice, thinking about benefits broadly.
- Identify the primary benefits of each Choice to be included on the Future Choices Benefits Matrix.

Exercise Work Product

- Future Choices Benefits Matrix—a summary of the primary benefits of each Future Choice

Post a photo or modestly elaborated record of the Team's whiteboard notes in the Team Meeting Notes section of the Decision Book and post a stand-alone version of the Future Choices Benefits Matrix in the Team Meeting Notes and Choices for the Future sections.

Following this exercise, Team members or staff may analyze the Choices further and refine the benefits profiles. New information can be brought back to the Team when the Benefits and Barriers Matrix is developed in Exercise 9-3.

The Team will develop a Success, Risk, and Values Profile (SRV Profile) in Chapter 12 as a qualitative comparison of the Choices. When Decision Makers convene to choose the path forward for the company, the Benefits and Barriers Matrix and the SRV Profile will be the primary summary comparisons of the Choices for the Future.

KEY TAKEAWAYS

1. Even if you believe you know the best initiative for addressing the company's challenge, pause and allow for the possibility that other options are worth considering.
2. Encourage unbounded and unconventional "all ideas are good ideas" thinking.
3. Don't ask for "great ideas." Start with lots of ideas, and then find the great ideas on the whiteboard.
4. *Create the Future* combines "all ideas are good ideas" creativity with disciplined reality.

PART 1: PREPARE THE COMPANY AND YOURSELF

PART 2: DEFINE THE CHALLENGE

PART 3: IMAGINE SUCCESS

PART 4: CREATE OPTIONS

PART 5: EVALUATE BARRIERS TO SUCCESS

PART 6: CHOOSE THE FUTURE

Chapter Topics

Execution Barriers—The Framework for Profiling Your Company Today

What Must Go Right?—Essential Requirements for Success

What Might Go Wrong?—Company Operations Today

What Will Happen?—Success Prospects

CHAPTER 9

EXECUTION BARRIERS
Getting there from here.

Imagination and creativity drove the Choices for the Future work. Disciplined practicality—can we get there from here?—drives the work of this chapter.

You identified possible Future Choices. The benefits you hope to capture from each Choice will only be realized if your company successfully executes the Choice's implementation plan. The CTF Team identifies and evaluates these execution risks in this chapter.

When you select a specific Future Choice as the path forward for your organization, you are also accepting a level of risk that the expected benefits will not be captured. You are choosing where on the low-to-high-risk spectrum you want to be. This chapter examines the execution barriers and develops a risk assessment for each Choice. If the Future Choices require competencies or resources significantly different from those of the organization today, understanding the execution barriers is an important reality check.

I outline a three-step process for identifying and describing the most important execution barriers and profile three Team exercises.

The chapter topics are:

Execution Barriers—The Framework for Profiling Your Company Today
Great ideas only have value to companies that can successfully execute them. I identify five business resources, practices, and operations categories that could be execution risks. As an example, I profile the execution barriers to growing to scale.

What Must Go Right?—Essential Requirements for Success
The Team identifies the essential requirements for success of each Future Choice. It then identifies the organization's capabilities, as they are today, which will be challenged by these requirements.

What Might Go Wrong?—Company Operations Today
The Team reviews the organization's resources, operations, and practices for potential execution barriers and develops a list of the Most Important Execution Risks.

What Will Happen?—Success Prospects
The Team estimates the probability of overcoming the most important execution barriers and profiles the Benefits and Barriers of each Choice.

We like to imagine what we could be in the future—rich, powerful, beautiful, famous, a few pounds lighter—and what we could be doing—playing with our kids, sailing across the Pacific. We spend less time thinking about what we are willing to do to achieve these goals. Running a business is no different. Successfully executing a new initiative is hard to do. Change is difficult. Before launching an initiative requiring your organization to do something different, be sure you understand the execution risks you are taking to capture the expected rewards.

Examining the execution barriers encourages you to make execution risk an explicit part of your decision-making. The following exercises help you decide whether to keep Future Choices with high execution risks on the table, modify them, or drop them. Leaders who make important decisions for their company while assuming someone else will figure out how to "make it work" are neglecting half their job.

Many, if not most, initiatives requiring significant change do not succeed. We, as individuals and as organizations, strongly resist change. You will improve your success prospects by taking a broad view of what can go wrong. Anticipate what could limit or block your plans and make dealing with those checkpoints part of your plan.

Divide the execution barriers analysis into three steps:
1. What must go right?
2. What might go wrong?
3. What will happen?

What must go right? looks at the essential requirements for success of each Future Choice. After profiling *what must go right?*, you may believe you have also

Leaders who make important decisions for their company while assuming someone else will figure out how to "make it work" are neglecting half their job.

---

identified *what might go wrong?* In some cases, they will be the same. But they may not be. Most acquisitions do not achieve the expected benefits, because unexpected integration barriers limit the performance of the combined operations.

While you can look at *what must go right?* and *what might go wrong?* at the same time, my recommendation is that you separate them. Carefully think about what is required for the new initiative to succeed. Then, look at *what might go wrong?* by identifying your organization's competencies that the new initiative will challenge. Additional execution barriers may emerge that did not surface from the *what must go right?* analysis. Identify each Future Choice's most important execution risks by drawing from *what must go right?* and *what might go wrong?*.

The objective of the analysis is not to prepare an execution plan for the Choices. The objective is to characterize the Future Choices by their execution risks using the information available and the Team's judgment. Understanding execution risk does not mean you, as a leader, should avoid risk. Elon Musk did not let execution risks stop him from growing Tesla from a start-up to a major automobile manufacturer or from growing SpaceX into a large scale commercial satellite company.

Make the best use of the Team's time by focusing on the characteristics of your company, as it is today, that are likely to be challenged by implementing each Future Choice. Adapt the exercises to the Choices you are considering. A limited execution barrier analysis may be sufficient if the Future Choices are a narrow range of options and mostly within the company's execution capability.

After the Team identifies the most critical execution risks, it will estimate the probability that the organization will overcome each execution barrier. The Team then prepares a summary of the Benefits and Barriers of each Choice.

> The future you imagine for your company might be well thought out and achievable by some company. The question is whether it is achievable by your company with its capabilities today.

EXECUTION BARRIERS
—THE FRAMEWORK FOR PROFILING YOUR COMPANY TODAY

The future you imagine for your company might be well thought out and achievable by some company. The question is whether it is achievable by your company with its capabilities today.

Successfully introducing a major new product to the market is difficult even when funding is not a limitation. Microsoft invested $1 billion to develop a smartphone called Kin. The product, targeting younger users, was dropped by Verizon in the United States six weeks after it was launched in 2010.

Also, consider the case of a Philadelphia-based company that has developed an innovative drug for treating Hodgkin's disease. Initial clinical trials were successful, and the founders believe the drug's market could approach $500 million annually. Before the company brings a commercial product to market, it must raise additional funding and conduct more clinical trials.

Potential investors are asking what the "go-to-market plan" will be if the remaining trials are successful. The founders created the company to pursue their vision for improving the lives of Hodgkin's patients. Though perhaps unsaid, the company is in the drug-development business. It has no commercial products, no sales force, no product distribution, no at-scale manufacturing, and no major banking relationships. If one of this company's Future Choices is manufacturing and selling its drug, marketing and sales, product distribution, and at-scale manufacturing are operational competencies to be developed. Creating those capabilities is a high-risk barrier to pursuing that business model.

Small, innovative drug-development companies create many commercially viable drugs. But they usually do not take them to market, because the barriers to becoming a successful drug manufacturing and sales company are too high. Selling the drug's IP to a large pharmaceutical company with these operational capabilities in place is usually the path taken by small drug-development company owners. If a company with manufacturing, sales, and distribution capabilities had developed the Hodgkin's drug, these would not be significant execution barriers.

Framework for Profiling Your Company

Every organization, every business, is unique, which is why each one is challenging, interesting, and maddening. But most companies can be profiled in five categories of competencies.

CATEGORIES OF BUSINESS COMPETENCIES
1. **Leadership**—leadership of the firm and cultural norms
2. **Business Model**—business model and strategic plan
3. **Products**—products and demand for products addressable by the company
4. **Finance**—capital strategy and access to capital
5. **Systems**—control of accounting and operations

Moving the company from where it is today to the company of the future may require changing some or all these core competencies. Use these business categories as a checklist for identifying competencies of your company today which are likely to be challenged by pursuing each Future Choice.

Growing to Scale—An Example of Execution Barriers

Successfully growing a small company to a significantly larger scale rarely happens. Growing larger by doing more of what you are already doing

---

Growing larger by doing more of what you are already doing usually does not work.

usually does not work. Growing to scale requires major changes to each of the five categories of business competencies. Firms that overcome each of these growth barriers are the ones that succeed.

As an illustration of how business practices and operations must change, here is a quick review of changes typical when moving from a start-up or small business to a larger business.

1. **Leadership**—The leadership and culture of a successful start-up or an established smaller company must change dramatically as the company grows to scale. For example, loyalty to the team must change to a culture of performance. Many start-up founders and key staff do not want to be in a more structured workplace and may not have the needed skills or temperament. And most staff, from the CEO to the production line, require different skills to grow. Some people can make this transition; many cannot.

2. **Business Model**—Start-ups and small businesses rely on intense collaboration with the customer and inexpensive yet highly skilled staff. The product or service is customized, and the production and delivery costs may be below market. The owner is often involved with selling and perhaps delivering the product. After the company has demonstrated it has satisfied a customer need, the question becomes, "What is the best business model?" For example, the company may have sold a hardware product but found that selling the service of using the hardware was a more scalable business model. A software company that was founded selling a children's app may change its business model to giving the app away and selling access to its customers like Google and Facebook are doing.

3. **Products**—Moving from low-volume, customized products to standardized, large-volume products is a major product strategy change. High-touch selling to a small number of clients does not scale to successful arms-length selling. To grow to scale, the company must deliver

its products in high quantities at a quality acceptable to the customers, with market-rate costs. Developing scalable sales and sales support channels—direct, distributors, or resellers—is a major growth challenge. Changing from a customer-centric business model to a production, cost-centric business that generates profits is the challenge.

4. **Finance**—Cash fuels growth. Selling equity and going into debt are the sources of cash. The financial strategy of an early-stage company must change when it grows to scale. The passion and commitment that convinced the founders, suppliers, early customers, and perhaps angel investors to take a chance and buy equity or extend credit or debt to fund the start-up will not alone bring institutional and professional investors and lenders to the table. New sources of capital to fund growth will require an attractive investment return for outside investors and a realistic plan for servicing debt.

5. **Systems**—Financial and operational control systems for a small company will not be adequate for a larger company. Start-ups and small companies can get by with simple accounting and operating systems with minimal need for integration and specialized IT infrastructure. Growth requires more robust integrated enterprise resource planning (ERP) and operating systems. With enough money and time, any transition to a different system's architecture is possible. Getting there is expensive, time-consuming, and risky.

Information Gathering before Engaging the Team

Before engaging the Team with the execution barriers analysis, do a preliminary scan of the five business competencies and identify the most likely execution risks for the Future Choices. With these potential challenge areas identified, gather information defining or characterizing the company's current capabilities.

Commission internal or consultant reports on relevant information such as sales estimates, financial projections, organizational changes, intellectual property prospects, and projected manufacturing costs. Compile the results in a format that highlights the company as it is today and is relevant to the Future Choices. The objective is to get this information in the Decision Book for the Team to consider before doing the execution barriers exercise.

WHAT MUST GO RIGHT?—ESSENTIAL REQUIREMENTS FOR SUCCESS

What must go right? is the first of three questions guiding the Team as it identifies the execution barriers for each Future Choice. *What might go wrong?* is the second question.

The team exercise companion to this book, *Create the Future—the Workbook,* profiles JFA Technology's search for growth opportunities based on its optical range-finding technology used for military products. One application for its technology is driverless cars. Products going into the consumer market must be manufactured at a cost point far lower than JFA's costs for low-volume military products. Product acceptance by the risk-averse auto industry and drastically reduced manufacturing costs are What Must Go Right requirements for success of this growth option. The Essential Requirements for Success Matrix developed by the JFA Team identified and profiled its high-risk execution barriers, as seen in the following illustration.

Essential Requirements for Success Matrix, Self-Driving Car Sensors

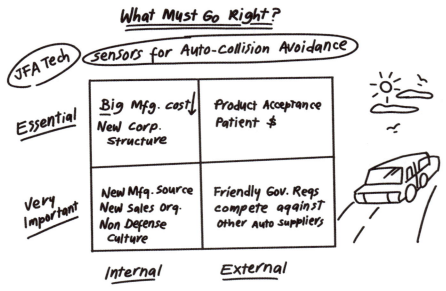

Exercise 9-1, "What Must Go Right: Essential Requirements for Success," asks *what must go right?* for each Future Choice to succeed and reach its goals. These must-go-right events can be changes to current company practices and operations or access to resources. They can also be events or decisions by others. Customer acceptance of a new product, hiring the right marketing manager, issuance of a patent, or a seller's acceptance of your purchase offer could be requirements for success. These requirements for success will be both essential and uncertain as to which way they will go.

Encourage a broad view of success requirements by outlining a Question Strategy and identifying categories of possible requirements for success. Exercise 9-1 uses a four-cell matrix Question Strategy that differentiates between "essential" and "important but not essential" success requirements and divides these into external and internal operational capability requirements.

The distinction between essential and important-but-not essential may not be clear, particularly at the beginning. Identify possible execution risks and post them on the whiteboard using a "best guess" as to which matrix cell is correct. With several success requirements posted, the Team will have a better understanding of what is "essential" and can adjust the postings. A cluster of important but not essential new capabilities could become an essential requirement for success. These categories will apply to most organizations. If other categories are a better Question Strategy for broadening your thinking, go for it.

Fill out the matrix by identifying performance levels the organization must achieve, external events that must happen, or access to funding or access to critical resources that must be secured. Each posted item should be important or essential to the success of a Future Choice. The result is a Requirements for Success Matrix.

After the Team posts possible success requirements, identify the Essential Requirements for Success by consensus. These will be the most critical and uncertain execution risks to be carried forward in the decision-making analysis. The result is a List of Essential Requirements for Success broken into Internal and External categories.

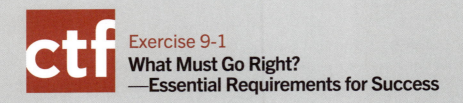

Exercise 9-1
What Must Go Right?
—Essential Requirements for Success

This exercise asks the question *What must go right?* for each Future Choice to succeed. The exercise identifies essential success requirements with uncertain prospects.

Exercise Steps

- On the whiteboard, draw a four-cell Success Matrix for each Future Choice with Essential and Important as the vertical scale and Internal and External as the horizontal scale.
- Identify internal resources, practices, and operations important to or essential for each Choice's success that are not company capabilities today and will be difficult to develop or acquire.
- Identify events or actions outside the company that must happen or must not happen, and there is uncertainty about their outcome.
- From the posted success requirements, identify (circle) the most essential success requirements for each Choice (List of Essential Requirements for Success).

Exercise Work Products

- Requirements for Success Matrix for each Future Choice showing important elements of the execution plan with a high level of success uncertainty
- List of Essential Requirements for Success identifying "must go right" elements of each Future Choice's implementation plan with a high level of success uncertainty separated into internal and external categories

Include a photo or modestly elaborated record of the Team's whiteboard notes in the Team Meeting Notes section of the Decision Book. Create cleaned up versions of the Requirements for Success Matrix and the List of Essential Requirements for Success for each Choice. File the Matrix and the List of Essential Requirements for Success as separate documents in the

Meeting Notes and Key Assumptions sections. The Team will use the List of Essential Success Requirements in the following exercises.

WHAT MIGHT GO WRONG?—COMPANY OPERATIONS TODAY

The journey begins where you stand today. Knowing the company today is the starting place for understanding the barriers to where you want to go tomorrow.

What might go wrong? is the second step of the execution barriers analysis. A realistic understanding of the success potential of a new initiative must include an evaluation of the company's operations as they are today, which are most likely to be challenged by the initiative.

Exercise 9-2, "What Might Go Wrong?—Company Operations Today," identifies the company's resources, operations, and practices, as they are today, which will be challenged by the Future Choices under consideration. The "Essential Requirements for Success" exercise identified execution risks but may not have identified all risks.

This exercise begins by identifying the company's current capabilities with a material uncertainty as to whether they can be upgraded or adapted to the requirements of the Future Choices. Use the five business competencies categories as a Question Strategy checklist for identifying execution barriers. Creating a general profile of the company and its capabilities is not the objective.

After completing the Company Operations Today analysis, combine the challenged company competencies with the Essential Requirements for Success. From the two lists, select the risks with the biggest impact on the success of the Future Choices and a high uncertainty as to their outcome. Uncertainty, in this case, means that the risk of failing to achieve the execution goal or requirement is high or you just don't know what will happen. The Team uses this final List of the Most Important Execution Risks to estimate the probability of overcoming each Choice's execution barriers in the following exercise.

As an illustration, consider the company whose leadership is considering options for upgrading its outdated manufacturing technology. Introducing robotics into the manufacturing process is one of the Future Choices. The

What Might Go Wrong?—Company Operations Today profile could include challenged capabilities such as:

- Outdated manufacturing lines or plants
- Labor contracts
- Critical staff skills
- Quality Control systems
- Access to capital

What Might Go Wrong?—Company Operations Today

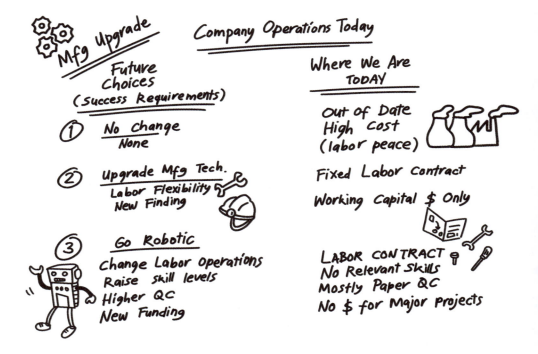

The Future Choices for a different company could be investing in product development to drive growth or, alternatively, selling the company to a strategic investor with better access to the capital needed for product development and sales development. In this case, the execution barriers analysis will include the company's financial and technical capabilities, which would be challenged by a costly product development effort, and also the financial and intellectual property profile, which would be needed to make the company an attractive acquisition prospect for a strategic buyer.

Culture, Values, and Risk Tolerance

> *Culture will trump strategy every time.*
> —Nilofer Merchant, *The New How*

There are numbers, and then there's how it works. Your company's risk tolerance and culture will be an important determinant of its prospects for successfully implementing a new initiative.

You can characterize an organization's culture by the beliefs, assumptions, values, and ways of interacting shared by most members. Smaller owner-run companies often have a minimal formal structure and rely on personal relationships among the core staff to get a wide range of functional work done. In other companies, the owner will be autocratic and make arbitrary decisions based on personal needs at the moment. These different cultures will profoundly influence what is achievable if the owner wants to change what the company is doing.

The autocratic company will be able to start a new initiative quickly but will not be successful for long if collaboration and cooperation are required. The "family culture" company will resist change and will probably need new leadership to grow to a larger scale.

Every business has a risk tolerance profile, even if not openly articulated. Cash on hand, debt levels, customer payment terms, and insurance coverage are expressions of risk tolerance. Leading a failed start-up is often seen as "education" and not a career stain in the U.S. entrepreneurial community. Other cultures attach personal failure and shame to a leader whose company or project fails. A highly risk-averse culture will have difficulty getting people to start new ventures or projects when failure is a real possibility.

When you and other Decision Makers meet on your own to decide which Future Choice to pursue, each of you will have their own understanding of the organization's culture when assessing the likelihood that a Choice will be successful. My recommendation is that you surface culture and risk tolerance as execution barriers and openly consider them as part of your evaluation of the Future Choices.

> **NOT PLANNING FOR SUCCESS—THE LAUNCH OF NETFLIX**
>
> Marc Randolph recounts his failure to understand the execution barriers to launching Netflix in his book *That Will Never Work*. Before Netflix, we went to a movie theater to see the latest movie or went to Blockbuster to rent or purchase a film on tape or DVD. The idea that we could rent the film on a DVD online, have it delivered by mail, and return it by mail was hard to believe. Randolph had difficulty convincing his mother to be an early investor.
>
> Randolph and the founding team gathered in a conference room to share the moment when the Netflix website went live for the first time. They had a connection to the website that would ring a bell when a customer ordered a DVD. Champagne was in an ice bucket.
>
> At 9 a.m. the site went live. After a few minutes, the bell rang. It rang again, and they opened the bottle of Champagne. More rings. Then silence. No ringing bell. Had their friends ordered a movie, and that was it?
>
> Eventually, the Netflix team discovered that an avalanche of customers signed onto the website hosted by a small server sitting on their desk. The server crashed. They had not anticipated the magnitude of their success and prepared to meet customer demand.

Identify company operations today which are major execution risks by doing Exercise 9-2, "What Might Go Wrong?" Include a photo or modestly elaborated record of the Team's whiteboard notes in the Team Meeting Notes section of the Decision Book. Create a cleaned-up List of the Most Important Execution Risks as a standalone document to include in the Meetings Notes and Judgment Calls sections.

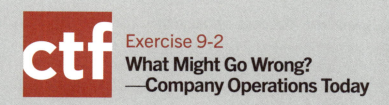

Exercise 9-2
What Might Go Wrong? —Company Operations Today

This exercise identifies and characterizes the company's current resources, business practices, and operations likely to be high execution risks. The most important execution risks are then selected from the Requirements for Success and Company Today risks.

Exercise Steps

- Outline a two-column table with column headings of Future Choices (Success Requirements) and Company Today. Post the first Choice with its Requirements for Success listed below.
- For each Requirement, post current capabilities in the Company Today column.
- Using the five categories of business competencies, ask if operations or capabilities of the company today are likely to be challenged by this Choice but are not listed as a Success Requirement. If so, post the required capability in the Choices column under a subheading of Operations Today. Characterize the company's current capabilities in the Company Today column.
- Ask if there are operations or practices reflecting the company's risk tolerance or culture that will be execution barriers.
- Repeat for each Choice.
- Ask which of the listed Requirements for Success plus the challenged Company Today competencies are the most important execution risks (circle).

Exercise Work Product

- List of the Most Important Execution Risks for each Future Choice, including a description of the company's relevant current capabilities

WHAT WILL HAPPEN?—SUCCESS PROSPECTS

The Essential Requirements for Success exercise asked, *What must go right?* The Company Operations Today exercise asked, *What might go wrong?* The next question is, *What will happen?*

Exercise 9-3, "What Will Happen?—Success Prospects," assesses the success prospects for overcoming each major execution barrier. This exercise allows Team members to share their judgments about the prospects for overcoming the execution barriers and learn how other members assess the risks. The exercise is an important reality check on the Team's assessment of the options on the table. The Team then develops a Benefits and Barriers Profile presenting the benefits and barriers of each Choice in a comparable format.

You have identified and described the most important execution barriers. Now, pose this question: "Taking everything you know and your personal experience into account, what do you believe is the probability the organization will successfully overcome this execution barrier?"

You are asking Team members to estimate the probability that the company will overcome each execution barrier. Neither you nor they know with certainty what will or will not happen. The execution barriers analysis is a complex topic with many elements and conflicting information. Team members are sharing their informed opinions with each other at that moment in time. And they learn from the reasoning of other Team members.

When the Decision Makers convene to choose the preferred Future Choice, they will, explicitly or implicitly, estimate the likelihood that the organization will overcome each execution barrier before selecting the path forward. This exercise is a "sum it all up" and "where we are now" check-in for the Team and the Decision Makers on the Team. Opinions about the execution risks may change, but this exercise asks for a show of hands at this point in time.

Understanding risk is the objective, not avoiding risk. Risk is part of almost every decision you make. When you choose the organization's future path, you are deciding how much risk of failure is acceptable. There is no right or wrong answer.

When deciding whether to pursue a Future Choice initiative, you and other Decision Makers will consider the risk of failure, the consequences of failure, and the benefits of success. And you are making the decision using your risk-tolerance filter. You could be saying, "This must work, or we will be out of business." Or, "Even if this does not work, we will learn some valuable lessons."

Understanding risk and weighing the expected costs against the probability that you will capture the potential benefits are part of your decision-making process. The same initiative will be a "bet the company" option for one firm and a "worth the risk for the possibility of a good investment return" for another.

When the Team estimates the probability that the organization will overcome an execution barrier, make the estimates anonymously. Allow Deciders on the Team to keep their estimates private at this point. Decision Makers can disclose their estimates if they choose. But keeping the Decider's feasibility estimates confidential gives them more latitude to change their opinion as the process continues and encourages others to offer different opinions.

The Team makes two rounds of estimates. The Team will learn from the first round and the following discussion. Some members may change their estimates after listening to the discussion. The second round of estimates is the Team assessment to be included in the Decision Book.

A second "sum it up" step is compiling a Benefits and Barriers Profile with a comparative display of the Benefits and Barriers of each Choice. The objective is a top-line display of the principal benefits of each Choice and the most important and uncertain risks of pursuing that Choice. The comparative profiles will be important briefing documents when the Decision Makers choose the go-forward Future Choice.

Using the goal of raising revenues 8 percent annually on average over the next four years as an example, the Benefits and Barriers Profile could look like the illustration on the next page.

Understanding risk is the objective. Avoiding risk is not the objective.

Benefits and Barriers Profile

Target ⇒ Grow revenue 8% annually

Choices	Benefits	Barriers
Ⓐ New product	Long term revenue + profits, New customer (EBITDA?)	Product dev., New product intro
Ⓑ Raise Sales + Marketing $	No Tech Risk, Grow revenue	
Ⓒ New Customer Categories	No tech risk, No new product risk, Long term revenue + profit	Success with new customers, New distribution channels

Take the Team through Exercise 9-3, "What Will Happen?—Success Prospects." Include a photo or modestly elaborated record of the Team's whiteboard notes in the Team Meeting Notes section of the Decision Book. File a cleaned-up and stand-alone Overcoming Execution Barriers Estimate and the Benefits and Barriers Profile in the Meeting Notes and Choices sections.

In most cases, the Team will have enough information about the Choices and their risk profile to form an opinion about the likelihood the organization will overcome each Barrier. In some cases, the Team will want to see a draft implementation plan for a high-risk element to understand the most challenging execution risks better.

In those cases, complete the exercise for the barriers the Team believes it understands. Outside the Team meeting, profile the implementation steps for the execution task in question, including research or experiments needed to define the risks better. This work might identify different ways to secure the benefits, along with cost and schedule estimates. This information could come back to the Team, or it could go directly to the Decision Makers for their consideration.

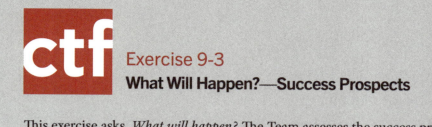

Exercise 9-3
What Will Happen?—Success Prospects

This exercise asks, *What will happen?* The Team assesses the success prospects for each execution barrier for each Future Choice. After making success estimates, the Team develops a Benefits and Barriers Matrix.

Exercise Steps

- Outline a table with column headings of Choices (Barriers), Success Estimate, and Comments. In the Choices column, list the Choices with their primary barriers below.
- Estimate the company's likelihood of successfully overcoming each barrier with a reasonable budget and time commitment. Record the estimates on slips of paper, using a 1 to 10 scale without the member's name. Post totals.
- Ask for the reasoning behind the estimates. Record keywords in the Comments column.
- Take a second vote. The results become the Overcoming Execution Barriers Estimate.
- Outline a table with column headings of Choices, Benefits, and Barriers.
- Post the Benefits from Exercise 8-3. Post the Barriers. Ask if the benefits and barriers of the Choices are fairly represented. If not, what is missing? When finalized, the results become the Benefits and Barriers Profile.

Exercise Work Products

- Overcoming Execution Barriers Estimate displaying the estimated likelihood each execution barrier will be overcome
- Benefits and Barriers Profile summarizing the primary benefits and barriers of each Future Choice

KEY TAKEAWAYS

1. The future you imagine for your company might be well thought out and achievable by some company. The question is whether it is achievable by your company with its capabilities today.
2. Culture will trump strategy every time.
3. Growing larger by doing more of what you are already doing usually does not work.
4. Leaders who make important decisions for their company while assuming someone else will figure out how to "make it work" are neglecting half their job.
5. Understanding risk is the objective. Avoiding risk is not the objective.

- PART 1: PREPARE THE COMPANY AND YOURSELF
- PART 2: DEFINE THE CHALLENGE
- PART 3: IMAGINE SUCCESS
- PART 4: CREATE OPTIONS
- **PART 5: EVALUATE BARRIERS TO SUCCESS**
- PART 6: CHOOSE THE FUTURE

Chapter Topics

Making Decisions with Incomplete Information

Thinking Fast and Thinking Slow

Key Assumption Options

CHAPTER 10

KEY ASSUMPTIONS
What you assume will happen and will not happen.

You create the future by the choices you make. Underlying your choices are assumptions about what you will accomplish, what others will do, and how the world will change.

Your choices also reflect assumptions about the consequences of your choices.

> *Before I sneak a cookie from the cookie jar on the shelf in my mom's kitchen, I make an assumption about whether my mother will notice the missing cookie. I also consider the consequences if she discovers I have taken a cookie.*

Before making important decisions, pause and ask, "Do I fully understand what I am assuming will happen?" An assumption is a choice. Choosing an assumption you are making when the outcome is uncertain is making a Judgment Call.

In this chapter I describe a Team exercise to identify the Key Assumptions underlying the success prospects of each Future Choice and alternative assumptions Decision Makers could make—Key Assumption Options.

The chapter topics are:

Making Decisions with Incomplete Information
Information underlying impactful decisions will always be incomplete. The basis for risk management is understanding the quality of what you know and the implications of different assumptions.

Thinking Fast and Thinking Slow
Giving yourself time to understand the implications of your choices will improve the quality of your decision-making.

Key Assumption Options

Before selecting the preferred Future Choice, identify Key Assumptions you will make about future events that will have a material impact on the success of the Future Choice. Imagine different assumptions you could make.

The Future Choices you are considering may be initiatives you can undertake with your organization's existing capabilities. Other than assuming the sales force will be motivated to push the product, you may not be making material assumptions underlying the success of the alternatives. In that case, the key assumption analysis may not be necessary.

MAKING DECISIONS WITH INCOMPLETE INFORMATION

You will choose your organization's future working with available information. The goal of the CTF process is to gather available data and estimates and organize the information in a format relevant to decisions you are making. The information will always be incomplete and conflicting.

Follow these steps for compiling the data available and managing the assumptions you will make:

1. Secure relevant current and historical data.
2. Define potential research or experiments which could reduce uncertainty.
3. Identify uncertain future events for which you must make an assumption.
4. Identify alternative assumptions you could make.
5. Specify the assumptions you are making.
6. Design the execution plan for the selected Future Choice to account for the quality of the available information and the uncertainty in the assumptions you are making.

The assumptions you are making and the quality of the available data will

---

An assumption is a choice.

have several levels of uncertainty:

- High confidence
- Reasonable estimates
- Educated guesses

Acknowledging the level of uncertainty in the incomplete and conflicting data and in your estimates is essential for risk assessment and risk management. Often, we make assumptions without realizing that they are estimates with their own uncertainty. Being clear that an assumption is also an estimate is necessary to understanding your decision's risk profile.

Market size, your existing market share, and the cost of future financing are values that are known or can be estimated with reasonable confidence. If you engage outside consulting support to gather data such as customer preferences, competitor financial profiles, and new customer conversion rates, the level of uncertainty in the estimates may be lower, but you will not eliminate uncertainty from the estimate.

Actions by others and events beyond your control may determine the success or failure of a new initiative. The estimates you make for future technology trends, the timing of the business cycle, and future tax policies are educated guesses at best. When choosing which initiative to pursue, you will make assumptions about future events beyond your control, and you will also assume the success of execution tasks over which you will have some, but not complete, control.

You will undertake initiatives relying on low-confidence estimates with more caution than decisions based on high-confidence estimates. Buying an established regional wealth-management practice in Seattle to expand your geographic coverage is more likely to succeed than building a new regional practice from scratch. The cost of buying an existing practice will be higher than building the practice from scratch, but the risks will be lower. The character of the performance and management reviews you set up for these different approaches to regional expansion will be completely different because they have different risk profiles.

THINKING FAST AND THINKING SLOW

An assumption is a prediction of an uncertain future event. An assumption is also a choice based on our best judgment.

You routinely make decisions using incomplete information about your organization, competitors, the marketplace, and the economy—explicitly or implicitly. Making assumptions is routine. We assume the sun will rise in the East tomorrow, and it usually does. Making assumptions in the face of uncertainty is necessary, even required.

In his book *Thinking, Fast and Slow*, Daniel Kahneman describes our mind as having two modes of decision-making. Most decision-making is Fast and essentially instinctive. Fast is our hard-wired mind. We make quick decisions based on assumptions and beliefs we don't take time to consider. Our Fast mind is impatient with the views of others when they are not driven by our sense of urgency and is even impatient with our own "lazy" Slow mind.

Our Slow mind will evaluate complex situations, but we seldom take time to use our Slow mind. That is why, when an important decision is on the table, it is important to take extra time to consider the assumptions you are making. Identify the assumptions you are making about events, access to resources, or level of performance. Weigh the impact of your assumptions on the success prospects for each Future Choice option. Identifying a critical assumption raises a red flag that says, "Important assumption here!" The red flag encourages you to pause. Consider the assumptions you could make and the implications of the assumption you do make.

This chapter encourages you to engage your Slow mind. You will identify where you are making an impactful assumption and identify different assumptions you could make.

Modeling and simulation analysis are tools for predicting the consequences of different assumptions. Simulation analysis predicts the consequences of different assumptions and scenarios on complex systems before you make a critical decision. In its many forms, simulation analysis is a

---

An assumption is a prediction of an uncertain future event.

Slow-Thinking tool for taking time to understand the assumptions you are making and the consequences of the choices you are considering.

Use simulation tools such as these to understand better the implications of alternative assumptions for the outcome of uncertain future events.

- Gaming the decision
- What-if analysis
- Running scenarios
- Stress testing
- Financial modeling
- War games

KEY ASSUMPTION OPTIONS

The best way to manage the risk in your assumptions is to be clear with yourself and your colleagues that you are making an assumption and to characterize the assumption's quality.

Before selecting which Future Choice to implement, you will make assumptions about how critical execution risks will play out. The CTF process encourages you to identify the assumptions you will make during the decision-making process and to be explicit about what assumptions you are making. Begin by identifying the assumptions. Then, communicate your assumptions to other Deciders. Sharing assumptions is an important dynamic of the group decision-making process.

Do the key assumption work in three steps:

- Identify important events, levels of performance, or access to resources for which you will make an assumption.
- Identify alternative assumptions you could make.
- Specify the assumption you are making.

Take your thinking through these three steps before every decision with underlying uncertainty. Identify the uncertainties for which you will make an assumption. Identify different assumptions you could make. Articulate the assumption you are making. You will make assumptions—consciously or unconsciously—whether you use the CTF approach or not. The value of this approach is that you are identifying the assumptions and openly considering them as part of your decision-making process.

Consider two examples of new initiatives where you might or might not let your Slow Mind thoroughly analyze and understand the risks.

Example 1

Your company is considering options for growing revenues for a core product. One option is acquiring a company with customers who are prospects for the product. The justification for the company's valuation rests on successfully cross-selling your product to the new customers. A Requirement for Success will be a high percentage of sales to the acquired company's customers.

You could make a "rule of thumb assumption" about the success of the post-acquisition cross-selling program before selecting or rejecting this option. A better approach would be to break down the elements of a successful cross-selling program. Include post-acquisition salesforce integration and product promotion to the new customers. You could identify the most problematic elements of the process and test different assumptions for those elements. Understanding the requirements for a successful cross-selling program with different levels of sales promotions to new customers would give you a better understanding of the acquisition option's risks.

Example 2

If selling the company is one of the Future Choices you are considering, the probability that senior staff will stay in place and cooperate with the company's leadership is an assumption worth identifying. For most initiatives, you will assume the company's staff will have normal turnover during the next year or two, and turnover is not worth highlighting. You will not make an explicit assumption about the level of turnover. But, in the case of wanting to sell the company as an operating business, retention of key leaders will be important determinant of the company's sales prospects. Leadership retention will be an assumption to include in the risk assessment.

Important Drivers Underlying the Execution Risks

Before exploring alternative assumptions about the company's ability to manage the execution risks, take one more look at whether all important execution risks have been identified. The Essential Success Requirements were developed by asking, *What must go right?* The Team identified Company Operations Barriers by asking, *What might go wrong?* The Key Assumptions List starts with the List of the Most Important Execution Risks and asks, *Are there important drivers underlying what must go right or what might go wrong that you should add to the List of the Most Important Execution Risks?*

If there is an underlying driver or influence on a Risk's severity or the prospects for overcoming it, add that driver to the Key Assumptions List.

As an example, Harvard University acquired a large parcel of land in the Allston section of Boston to build a $1 billion engineering and applied science complex. Access to financing was certainly an Essential Requirement for Success. The University made assumptions about sources of capital and their costs and assumed income would be available from its endowment. An underlying driver of these assumptions was the condition of the financial markets. Because Harvard has such a large endowment, it may not have considered financing to be a Major Execution Risk.

Construction started on the new engineering complex shortly before the financial crisis of 2008. Harvard's assumptions about access to capital—perhaps unspoken—were not correct. The University stopped construction on the site in 2009 and did not resume construction until 2019. If Harvard cannot predict where its funding is coming from, be humble about your predictions.

The Egg Business—Execution Risks and Key Assumptions

Look at the egg business as a more down-to-earth example of how

Major Execution Risks, underlying drivers of risk, and Key Assumptions work together.

The egg business depends on hens laying eggs. If hens do not lay eggs, there is no egg business. An Execution Risk is uncertainty about how many eggs the hens will lay every month. A farmer considering entering the egg business will make an assumption about the number of eggs the hens will lay—the hen's productivity. Hen productivity is a Key Assumption. An underlying driver of this Assumption, and therefore an Execution Risk, is whether the rooster will crow at sunrise. Some say that hens will not lay eggs if the rooster does not crow at sunrise.

The number of days the rooster crows at sunrise drives hen productivity. The farmer must make an assumption as to how many days each month the sun will rise in the East and there will be no clouds so the rooster will see the sun rising. Those assumptions are underlying drivers of hen productivity.

A business analyst could create a model estimating the sun's probability of rising in the East and the probability of sunny days in this location. The Key Assumptions for the egg business would include:

- Sun rising in the East
- Sunny days
- Rooster crowing at dawn
- Hen productivity after the rooster crows

(My family had chickens when I was small, and my mother sold eggs to British Overseas Airways. My job as a four-year-old was to collect the eggs. I remember the warmth of the chickens as I reached under them to gather the eggs, and I remember the wire basket for holding the eggs.)

The following illustration identifies these Key Assumptions. Whether the hens will be laying eggs is the top Execution Risk and a Key Assumption. Whether the sun will rise in the East and the day will be sunny or cloudy are underlying Key Assumptions of the egg business.

Key Assumptions, Egg Business

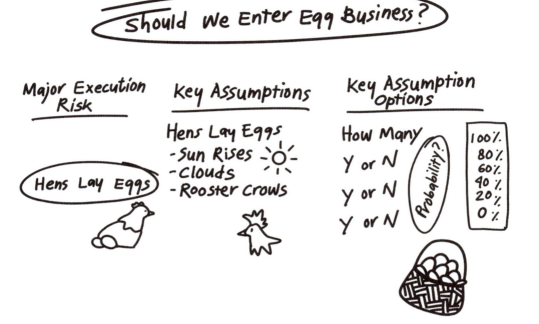

Exercise 10-1, "Key Assumption Options," identifies Key Assumptions underlying the success prospects of each Future Choice. For each assumption about how a critical element of the execution plan will play out, the Team identifies a range of assumptions that Decision Makers could make. These assumption alternatives are the Key Assumption Options.

This exercise puts different assumptions you could make in front of you and other Decision Makers. If you wait until the moment you must decide which Future Choice to pursue, you will give less thought to the assumption options than the Team can provide by looking at the question separately.

Start the Key Assumptions list with the Major Execution Risks. "Will this Execution Risk be overcome or not?"

The List of Major Execution Risks may include all underlying drivers of the high-risk execution barriers, but significant risks may not be included.

Events, performance levels, access to resources, decisions by outside actors, economic and financial market developments, and many other variables with uncertain outcomes could be significant risks. The Team may not have included these for any number of reasons. Encourage a discussion exploring whether the Team should add underlying drivers of the Execution Risks to the list of risks worth highlighting and to the Key Assumptions List. Capture the value of the exercise by asking the question.

After you identify where you are making a Key Assumption, develop a range of possible outcomes for each execution risk. These alternative outcomes are Key Assumption Options. The Options are different assumptions you and other Decision Makers could make for each important and uncertain event impacting the success of a Future Choice. Think about total sales revenues versus the cost of the new product to the consumer as an example.

When you and other Decision Makers meet to choose the preferred Future Choice, you will make assumptions about regulatory approvals and total revenue levels. The Key Assumptions List and the List of Major Execution Risks compile and display comparative information you will use when selecting between the Future Choice alternatives. These assumptions will be foundational to your selection of the preferred Future Choice.

Putting alternative assumptions on the table for you to consider helps you be clear to yourself that you are making a choice when you make an assumption—you have options. In this exercise, the Team gives you a clear view of assumptions you could make and relates the assumptions to the Future Choice's potential success.

If a risk analyst is on your Team, here is a suggestion you would hear. Making an assumption does not mean that outcome will happen. Something different might happen. Consider setting up a progress-monitoring and exceptions-reporting system during the Choice's execution. Early discovery that an important assumption was wrong allows for faster adjustments to the execution plan. If one possible assumption only has a 1% or 2% chance of happening but that development would blow up the company, you can assume it will not happen. But you should carefully watch for signs that it is happening and prepare contingencies for what to do if it does happen.

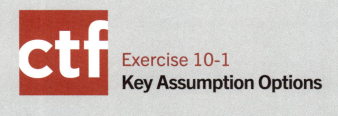

Exercise 10-1
Key Assumption Options

This exercise identifies Key Assumptions underlying your potential success assessment of each Choice for the Future. With the Key Assumptions identified, the Team identifies a range of alternative assumptions. These are different assumptions Decision Makers could make when evaluating which Future Choice to select as the preferred path forward. The alternative assumptions are the Key Assumption Options.

Exercise Steps

- Outline a three-column matrix with headings of Execution Risks, Assumptions, and Options.
- In the left column, write the first Choice as a topic heading. List its Major Execution Risks below the Choice.
- The first entry in the Assumption's column will be whether the organization will overcome the Execution Risk.
- Identify underlying performances, resources, and events that will be important drivers of the Execution Risks for which the Decision Makers must make a performance assumption. List these in the Assumption's column across from the corresponding Execution Risk.
- From the list of Execution Risks and their underlying drivers, ask which are important enough to be on the Key Assumptions List. A Key Assumption should be impactful enough to change a Choice's prospects of successful implementation materially.
- For each consensus Key Assumption, post in the Options column a range of assumptions Decision Makers could make about its outcome or level of performance.
- Repeat the process for each Choice.
- The consensus assumptions become the Key Assumption List for each Future Choice. The Key Assumptions List and the possible

options for each assumption become the Key Assumption Options list.

Exercise Work Products
- Key Assumption List for each Choice for the Future
- Key Assumption Options listing alternative assumptions Deciders could make about future events and performance levels essential to the success of each Future Choice

A photo or modestly elaborated version of the Team's whiteboard notes from Exercise 10-1 will go in the Team Meeting Notes section of the Decision Book. Create cleaned-up and stand-alone versions of the Key Assumptions List and the Key Assumption Options list and file these in the Meeting Notes section. The Key Assumptions List and the Key Assumption Options also go in the Key Assumptions section of the Book. The Key Assumption Options list goes in the Decisions to Be Made section as well.

The Key Assumption Options exercise could be done for six Future Choices, each with four Major Execution Risks. Keep it simple. Focus on the essential assumptions with a big impact on the choices under consideration.

KEY TAKEAWAYS

1. Underlying your choices are assumptions about what you will accomplish, what others will do, and how the world will change.
2. An assumption is a prediction of an uncertain future event.
3. An assumption is a choice.
4. The best way to manage the risk in the assumptions you make is to be clear with yourself and your colleagues that you are making an assumption and to characterize the assumption's quality.

PART 1: PREPARE THE COMPANY AND YOURSELF

PART 2: DEFINE THE CHALLENGE

PART 3: IMAGINE SUCCESS

PART 4: CREATE OPTIONS

PART 5: EVALUATE BARRIERS TO SUCCESS

PART 6: CHOOSE THE FUTURE

Chapter Topics

Decision Agenda

A Decision Tree

Decision Agenda Exercise

CHAPTER 11

DECISION AGENDA
What decisions must I make?

As the leader, your job is to make decisions—to make choices. When you began the Create the Future work, you asked, or should have asked:

What decisions must I make?

This chapter encourages you to identify and anticipate the most important decisions you and other Decision Makers must make.

The chapter topics are:

Decision Agenda
A Decision Agenda identifies key decisions to be made by Decision Makers and those outside the organization, leading to selecting the go-forward Future Choice.

A Decision Tree
A Decision Tree displays the sequence and network of these decisions.

Decision Agenda Exercise
The Team develops a Decision Agenda approved by the Decision Makers on the Team.

Making a decision—a simple concept but a complex event. Successful leaders see decision-making as a process. Their job is to manage the process as well as make decisions.

When presented with an important decision, you should be asking:

- What decisions must I make?
- When must I make the decisions?
- What decisions will others make that will impact the choices I have?

Successful leaders see decision-making as a process. Their job is to manage the process as well as make decisions.

DECISION AGENDA

The Decision Agenda is your decision-making guide. The Agenda identifies and defines the decisions you must make, ending with choosing which Future Choice to pursue. The Decision Agenda has two elements:

- ▸ List and description of each important decision to be made
- ▸ A Decision Tree defining the network of decisions to be made

Preparing a Decision Agenda empowers you as a leader. Defining the decisions to be made brings clarity to the choices that must be made and to your role in making those choices. Defining the network of decisions strengthens your control of the decision-making process.

The Decision Tree profiles the network of related and contingent decisions you and others will make. Decisions or events outside the organization that will impact the Choice's success prospects are included on the Tree so your decisions are understood in context.

CTF exercises usually record the Team's consensus or majority views on a topic. Decision Makers consider these Team recommendations when making their decisions. The Decision Agenda exercise profiled in this chapter asks the Deciders on the Team to approve the description of the decisions to be made. The result is a decision agenda that can be directly used by the Decision Makers to select the go-forward Future Choice.

The Decision Agenda will not prescribe what choices to make. But the process of creating a Decision Agenda is an opportunity for you and other Decision Makers to develop your thinking about the decisions you must make and to hear other Team member's views about the decisions to be made.

You may not want to commit to a specific formulation of the decision process and may want to keep the Decision Agenda as a recommendation by the Team. That approach can work, but settling on the decision steps you will use to select the preferred Future Choice prepares you to make the decisions and finalizes the plan for making the decisions.

A DECISION TREE

When choosing the future path for your organization, you are seldom making a simple Yes-or-No decision. Often a sequence of related decisions is required. Select A or B. If you select A, choose C or D. If you select B, choose E or F.

A Decision Tree outlines a network of related decisions. It is a tool for identifying the decisions and their connection to each other. You will use the decision tree tool when the decisions to be made are complex and multilayered.

In the CTF context, the Tree will display the network of decisions to be made by you or the committee or board of Decision Makers and, in some cases, those outside the company that will materially impact the success prospects of the Future Choice options. The Tree will also include discovery and feedback loops, if appropriate. The Tree highlights important Go/No-Go choices and helps you prepare for and focus on what you must decide at each moment in the overall sequence of decisions.

In some cases, actors outside the organization or leaders in the company who are not Decision Makers for this CTF work will make impactful decisions. If those decisions are within the same timeframe as the decisions to be made by the Decision Makers and they will determine the options available to the Deciders, include them on the Decision Tree. The Decision Tree identifies and clarifies what decisions will impact the Future Choices and who will make them.

With the essential decisions identified, the Team can identify initiatives that can be undertaken to prepare for making the decisions. If the Future Choices include new products with different success risks, you may want to prepare a market test proposal so it is available for the Team meeting. Anticipating information requests or experiments that could clarify

---

Preparing a Decision Agenda empowers you as a leader.

the decisions to be made or reduce their uncertainty will limit delays in the decision process.

Defining each Future Choice does not prepare you for the decision process you will experience. A Decision Tree profile of the network of decisions you and your leadership team must make to select the preferred Future Choice will encourage you to prepare to make the decisions. Do not overly complicate the decision tree analysis. The goal is to profile the network of essential Go/No-Go decisions and identify preparation that will help you make better decisions.

A Decision Tree Example

You might say, "I want to grow this company and get it to the point where I can sell it. I must choose a growth path that will make the company interesting to a buyer in three years."

The CTF process elements are:

- **Success:** Sell the company.
- **Goal:** Grow the company to a size where it can be sold.
- **Future Choices:** Identify growth initiatives.
- **Barriers/Assumptions:** Evaluate execution risks of the growth initiatives.
- **Decision:** Select the preferred growth initiative with an acceptable level of risk.

At this point in the CTF process, the Team will have identified and evaluated growth initiatives—the Choices for the Future. The Team's next contribution is to clarify the decisions you must make from this moment in time through to when you select the company's growth initiative. The Decision Tree portrays the sequence of decisions, and each individual decision or choice in the sequence is a Decision Node.

Suppose one of the growth initiatives has a high risk of failure. That Choice may not get serious consideration unless an experiment is run to reduce the implementation uncertainty. One decision you must make is whether to run the experiment and wait for the results or move ahead without the experiment.

The Decision Tree illustration profiles the network of decisions leading up to selecting the best future growth option.

Decision Tree

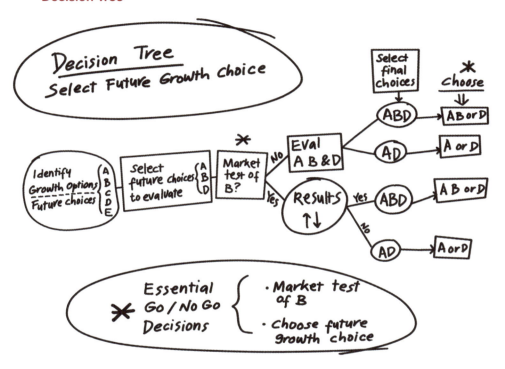

DECISION AGENDA EXERCISE

When you are facing an important decision, ask the following sequence of questions:

- ▶ What decisions must I make?
- ▶ What do I need to know before I decide?
- ▶ Can we run an experiment to clarify the options?
- ▶ When do I have to make a decision?
- ▶ Is this a decision only I can make?

The Decision Agenda will strengthen your confidence. You will know which decisions you must make and when you must make them.

As part of your preparation for the CTF work, you had a homework assignment. Exercise 1-1, "Your Motivation for Using CTF," asked you to identify the decisions you hope CTF will help you make (*Leader's Initial Decisions to Be Made Statement*). Your description of these decisions starts the Decision Agenda work.

With your *Initial Decisions to Be Made Statement* in hand, take the Team through Exercise 11-1, "Decision Agenda." The Team begins this exercise by listening to your description of the decisions to be made. The Team then develops a consensus Decision Tree, if applicable, and describes the most important decisions. You and other Deciders on the Team are asked if the draft Decision Agenda is acceptable. Does this formulation represent your expectations for the network of decisions to be made and accurately describe the decisions? If not, work through adjustments to the Decision Tree and the important decision descriptions to make them acceptable to the Decision Makers.

Convening the Team to help define the decisions you must make is similar to making sure you are solving the right problem. Your Leader's Initial Decisions Statement probably needs elaboration and clarification and does not include a decision tree of related decisions. Begin the Team's work by giving a verbal description of your Initial Decisions Statement. A verbal description will better communicate your openness to the Team's contributions than will distributing a written "official" statement of the decision to be made. The value of this exercise to you is learning the Team's perspective on the decisions. And the exercise may identify preparation work you should initiate before making the decisions.

Exercise 11-1
Decision Agenda

This exercise identifies important decisions to be made by Decision Makers and those outside the organization leading up to the go-forward Future Choice selection. The Team outlines a Decision Tree, if applicable, and identifies and describes the primary decisions to be made.

Exercise Steps

- The senior Leader offers an "initial description" of the primary decisions the Decision Makers will make when preparing for and selecting the preferred Future Choice. Post keyword descriptions of the decisions.
- Ask for clarification questions on the decisions and the issues to be resolved.
- Ask if additional decisions will be important when preparing to select the Future Choice and selecting the preferred Choice.
- Outline a Decision Tree displaying the network of decisions by company leaders and outside Decision Makers, including feedback and experimental loops.
- Develop a consensus Decision Tree of important decisions acceptable to the Decision Makers.
- List the decisions on the Decision Tree with a description of each acceptable to the Decision Makers.
- Identify preparation that will be required or helpful prior to making the decisions.

Exercise Work Products

- Decision Agenda including a Decision Tree and a list of the Decisions to Be Made
- Decision Preparations List—special preparation prior to decision meetings

A photo or modestly elaborated recording of the Team's whiteboard notes will go in the Team Meeting Notes section of the Decision Book. Create cleaned-up and stand-alone versions of the Decision Tree and the Decisions to Be Made lists, and file these in the Meeting Notes section. The Decision Tree and the Decisions to Be Made list also go in the Decisions to Be Made section.

> **KEY TAKEAWAYS**
> 1. Making a decision—a simple concept but a complex event.
> 2. As the leader, your job is to make decisions—to make choices.
> 3. Engage the Team to help you be clear what decisions you must make.
> 4. Successful leaders see decision-making as a process. Their job is to manage the process as well as make decisions.

PART 1: PREPARE THE COMPANY AND YOURSELF
▼
PART 2: DEFINE THE CHALLENGE
▼
PART 3: IMAGINE SUCCESS
▼
PART 4: CREATE OPTIONS
▼
PART 5: EVALUATE BARRIERS TO SUCCESS
▼
PART 6: CHOOSE THE FUTURE

Chapter Topics

What Have We Learned?
Do We Need to Know More?

Success, Risk, and Values

Team Recommendations—
Key Assumptions and Future Choices

CTF Team Report—Decision Book and Decision Package

CHAPTER 12

PREPARE TO CHOOSE
Understand the "meaning" of your decision.

Create the Future is about making decisions. Making a decision is choosing.

Before you and other Decision Makers convene to evaluate the Future Choices for the company and select a path forward, do a final check on whether you are ready to choose.

This chapter asks you to step back and think about what you have learned about the challenge facing you and about the possible solutions you have identified. The Team estimated the costs and expected benefits of each Future Choice. In this chapter, I outline four exercises the Team, or the Decision Makers by themselves, can use to profile the "meaning" of the decisions you will make.

The chapter topics are:

What Have We Learned? Do We Need to Know More?
Consider what you have learned. Ask whether you are addressing the right problem and have defined the best solutions.

Success, Risk, and Values
Define the meaning of each Future Choice by developing its Success, Risk, and Values Profile.

Team Recommendations—Key Assumptions and Future Choices
The Team makes its recommendations for the Key Assumptions and ranks the Choices for the Future options if these recommendations are valuable to the Decision Makers.

CTF Team Report—Decision Book and Decision Package
The Decision Book is the Team's consultant report to the Decision Makers. The Decision Package profiles the decisions to be made and becomes part of the Decision

Makers' meeting agenda.

You may or may not include non-Deciders in this chapter's exercises. If the company owner or CEO will make the final decisions and the Team is the organization's leadership, the Team's participation in this chapter's exercises can be a valuable contribution to the Decision Makers' deliberations. If the Team is a board of directors or executive committee plus one or two outside contributors, limiting the exercises in this chapter to the Decision Makers may be the best use of Decider's time.

If the CTF Team is only Decision Makers, consider assembling a small group of staff and perhaps outside advisors and briefing them on the options being considered. Ask the group for its feedback by taking them through the exercises in this chapter. New insights may come from the group. Adding this step to the process may or may not be feasible for confidentiality, time, or cost reasons. But it is an option to consider if feedback from outside the Decider group would be helpful.

If Decision Makers alone will be doing the Prepare to Choose work, do not do the Team Recommendation Exercises, 12-3 and 12-4. Decision Makers alone may want to do the Do We Need to Know More and SRV Profile exercises. If so, these exercises become the first phase of the decision-making process completed in Chapter 13, when Deciders disclose their personal perception of the Choice's SRV Profiles and the Key Assumptions they will make. Get legal counsel's advice on what documentation should be retained or discarded if this work is part of an official board or executive committee meeting.

The exercises in this chapter, as written, assume they are done as Team exercises, including non-Deciders. If Deciders are the only participants, adjust the exercise steps to reflect your circumstances.

WHAT HAVE WE LEARNED? DO WE NEED TO KNOW MORE?

Create the Future Thinking encourages you to ask, "What are we learning? Do we understand the problem we are trying to solve or the options we have in a new way?"

When a colleague says, "Before you do that, have you thought about . . . ?" often our reaction is, "Don't complicate this. I just want to get this done!" A year later, a week later, we are kicking ourselves. "Why didn't I think of that?!"

The Team created the Future Choices. It evaluated the execution risks of each Future Choice and identified significant assumptions underlying the success potential of the Choices. Pausing to ask, "What have we learned?" is a healthy and powerful challenge question. Exercise 12-1, "What Have We Learned? Do We Need to Know More?," asks the Team to consider whether it is solving the right problem and whether the Future Choices are the best possible solutions to the problem. Courage is required to ask, "Have we gotten this right?"

Asking these questions is the value of the exercise. These open-ended questions may go nowhere. The answer could be, "We know a lot more, and we are confident that we understand the problem. We also have options to pursue that can get us where we need to be." That is great! But another answer could be, "Our understanding of the goals we set has changed, and we want to look at more options before choosing the final initiative to pursue."

Ask these questions with the understanding that the Team is your advisor. Recognizing the value of their insights and deciding what to do with them are your responsibilities.

This exercise also asks if additional information will reduce the uncertainty about how the Future Choices will play out. More information is always helpful, but limit additional information gathering to data that will clarify the differences between the Choices. Running a limited experiment on potential customer preferences could be a recommended next step.

Time and resources limit every organization and leadership team. Where to place limits on the Team's preparation work is an important decision you must make. Exercise 12-1 will help you choose the stopping point—when you believe the Team has gathered the relevant available information and profiled the Choices enough to understand their risk/reward profile and their implications for the organization.

The Team is your advisor. Recognizing the value of their insights and deciding what to do with them are your responsibilities.

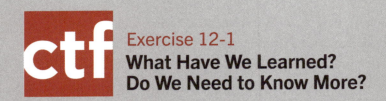

Exercise 12-1
What Have We Learned? Do We Need to Know More?

With the Key Assumption exercises completed, this exercise asks the Team what it has learned. Is the Team solving the right problem, and do the Choices address the problem? Will limited research or experiments reduce uncertainty?

Exercise Steps

- Building on the Key Assumptions work, ask what has been learned about the opportunity or threat facing the company that was not known earlier.
- Ask what has been learned about the Future Choices under consideration and their execution risks.
- In light of what the Team has learned, ask if the Choices are addressing the right Challenge. If not, what is the right formulation of the Challenge—the opportunity or threat?
- Are the Future Choices the best options for addressing the Challenge? If not, what other options should be considered?
- If there is substantial doubt on either of these points supported by the Decision Makers, define steps to reexamine them.
- In light of the execution risks, ask what limited information gathering or experiments the company should do to reduce the risks or narrow the range of uncertainty.

Exercise Work Products

- What We Learned about the Challenge and the Choices for the Future
- Information to be gathered or experiments to be run to reduce risk, if any

A photo or modestly elaborated recording of the Team's whiteboard notes will go in the Team Meeting Notes section of the Decision Book. Create cleaned-up and stand-alone versions of What We Learned and the additional information or experiments requested, and file these in the Team Meeting Notes section.

The conclusion of this exercise may be, "There are risks and uncertainty, and they are part of being in this business." Or a new insight may have emerged that was not there before. Asking the question is an opportunity for the insight to come forward.

SUCCESS, RISK, AND VALUES PROFILE
The Benefits and Barriers Matrix developed in Chapter 9 organized the top-level quantitative characteristics of each Choice, including the financial benefits, cost estimates, and primary execution barriers. Beyond the quantitative and execution profiles, the Choices for the Future may have other differentiating characteristics important to the Decision Makers. These characteristics can give "meaning" to choosing one future path rather than another.

When President Kennedy set the goal that the United States would land a man on the moon in ten years, he directed NASA to build its headquarters in Cambridge, Massachusetts, his home state. Many city blocks in East Cambridge were acquired and cleared of buildings. After Kennedy's assassination, Lyndon Johnson became president. He overrode Kennedy's decision and made Houston, Texas, his home state, NASA headquarters. If President Johnson had not moved NASA to Houston, the call from Apollo 13 would have been, "Cambridge, we have a problem."

For both Presidents Kennedy and Johnson, the deciding factor when choosing where to locate the NASA headquarters was the economic benefits NASA would bring to their home states.

Values like these drive many decisions. Initiatives with big potential will succeed or falter on the unspoken preferences, hopes, and fears of those

---

What are we learning? Do we understand the problem we are trying to solve or the options we have in a new way?

Initiatives with big potential will succeed or falter on the unspoken preferences, hopes, and fears of those involved.

involved. Before beginning the decision-making discussions, have an open conversation about "the meaning" of the Future Choices to you and other Decision Makers.

The Success, Risk, and Values Profile (SRV Profile) is a format for capturing and displaying the primary qualitative characteristics of the Choices and their "meaning." The SRV Profile and the Benefits and Barriers Matrix are the principal comparative summaries of the Future Choices.

Exercise 12-2, "Success, Risk, and Values Profile," asks the Team to characterize each Future Choice. This exercise develops Team consensus SRV Profiles to be considered by the Decision Makers. If Deciders are the only participants, the result is a set of consensus Decider SRV Profiles that feed into Exercise 13-2, "Characterize the Choices for the Future."

The SRV Profile categories and examples are:

- **Success**—What would this Choice accomplish and what would be its "meaning" to the principal stakeholders?

- **Risk**—Will we be managing "normal and acceptable" risk or "highly uncertain and unpredictable" risk?

- **Values**—Does the Choice express the values of the company, its leadership, and its owners? How will the Choice impact the shareholders and other major company constituencies?

Earlier exercises identified most, if not all, of these characteristics. The SRV Profile compiles that information in a comparative format. The SRV Profile and the Benefits and Barriers Matrix overlap to some degree, but the SRV Profile captures more of the character of the Choices. In contrast, the Benefits and Barriers Matrix captures more of the quantifiable characterization of the Choices.

Use a broad meaning of "values" in the SRV Profile. Many business decisions are expressions of values. These values could include where to set the balance of risk and reward, maintaining family ownership, or the aspirational statement of growing shareholder value. The Success work of Chapter 6 may also have identified "values" company owners want to express by the company's operations such as reducing its carbon footprint. Include these values, if applicable.

This exercise develops a consensus SRV Profile of each Choice supported by most Team members. The SRV Profile becomes a common language for describing the Team's and each Decider's qualitative assessment of the Choices. The Team consensus profiles are advisory recommendations to the Decision Makers. If there is substantial disagreement with the consensus view, the profile can include the alternative views.

Success, Risk, and Values Profile

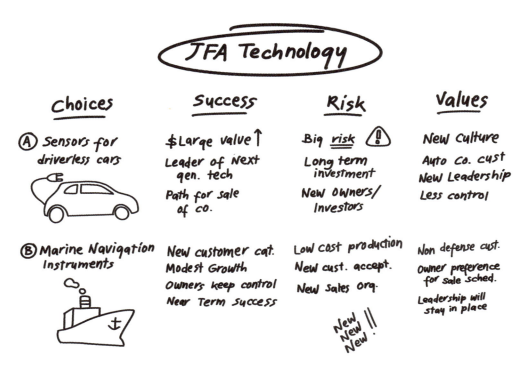

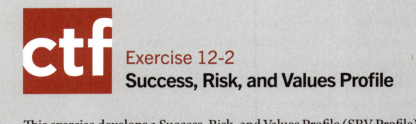

Exercise 12-2
Success, Risk, and Values Profile

This exercise develops a Success, Risk, and Values Profile (SRV Profile) summarizing the qualitative characteristics of the Future Choices and puts the information in a comparative format. The exercise may be done by the full Team, including non-Decision Makers, or by Decision Makers alone.

Exercise Steps

- On the whiteboard, post four columns. List the Choices in the left column. Other columns are Success, Risk, and Values.
- Beginning with Choice #1, ask the Participants to post a keyword description of Success other than achieving the established goals. Describe the Risk profile of the Choice. Identify Values the Choice expresses, supports, or undermines.
- Profile each Choice by its Success, Risk, and Values. Participants may describe the Choices differently, and these differences will be reflected in the keywords.
- Starting with Choice #1, ask the Participants which of the keyword descriptions are supported by most members. Circle the consensus descriptors. Repeat for each Choice.
- If members have different points of view, those differences can be noted on the profile. The profiles will be more valuable as summary comparisons if non-consensus opinions are limited to consequential and firmly held differences.

Exercise Work Product

- Success, Risk, and Values Profile of each Choice for the Future

A photo or modestly elaborated recording of the whiteboard notes will go in the Team Meeting Notes section of the Decision Book. Create cleaned-up and stand-alone versions of the SRV Profiles and file them in the Team Meeting Notes section. The Profiles will also go in the Decisions to Be Made section.

TEAM RECOMMENDATIONS
—KEY ASSUMPTIONS AND FUTURE CHOICES

If the CTF Team includes members who are not Deciders, the Decision Makers must decide whether to ask the non-Deciders for their recommendations on Key Assumptions and which Future Choice to pursue. Non-Decision Maker involvement in the decision-making process could take different forms including:

- No involvement. No information on decisions made.
- No participation in the decision-making process but reconvened after decisions are reached to learn the results and "celebrate" with the Decision Makers.
- Recommend which Key Assumptions to make.
- Recommend which Choice for the Future to pursue.
- Witness Decision Maker deliberations.

If the company owner or CEO will make the final decisions and the Team is the organization's leadership, the full Team's recommendations on Key Assumptions and the preferred Future Choice could be valuable to the Decider.

Engaging the Team in the decision-making process can also convey a helpful message. You did not assemble the Team to represent the company's constituencies, but, in a rough sense, it does. Deciders represent the shareholders. Senior staff, future leaders, and outside advisors may be on the Team. Communications with these non-Decider Team members and their involvement with the Decision Makers' deliberations are effectively engagement with the company's constituencies.

But there are circumstances when the recommendations of non-Deciders will not be helpful. And there are circumstances when the decision-making deliberations must be kept confidential from non-Decision Makers. The arguments for and against asking for the full Team's recommendations when the Team includes non-Deciders are summarized in the following table.

ASKING FOR NON-DECISION MAKER RECOMMENDATIONS

Benefits	Drawbacks
COMMUNICATE INTEREST IN NON-DECIDER VIEWS	CONFIDENTIAL INFORMATION CANNOT BE SHARED
NON-DECIDER VIEWS ARE A FACTOR TO BE CONSIDERED	DECISION MAKERS MAY NOT WANT TO REVEAL PREFERENCES TO NON-DECIDERS
DECISION MAKERS WILL LEARN FROM NON-DECIDERS	DECISION MAKERS MAY SELECT CHOICES NOT RECOMMENDED BY THE NON-DECIDERS

Decision Makers might decide to ask for Team recommendations on Key Assumptions but not the Future Choice selection. They may want both recommendations or neither. Hearing different views is always helpful, but the requirements of the issues at hand and the company's circumstances may not support the non-Decider's involvement in the decision-making process.

Exercise 12-3, "Key Assumptions—Team Recommendations," guides the Team through the steps for making Key Assumption recommendations. This form of the exercise keeps the recommendations of each Team member confidential so the Decision Makers on the Team can express their views without revealing or committing to a position. Conversely, Decision Makers may want to have an open conversation about the recommendations and choose not to use the secret ballot voting described in this version of the exercise.

If the Decision Makers decide not to ask for non-Decider Key Assumption recommendations, skip this exercise.

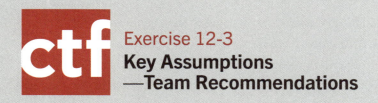

Exercise 12-3
Key Assumptions —Team Recommendations

In this exercise, the Team recommends which Key Assumptions to make when choosing the go-forward Future Choice for the company.

Exercise Steps

- Distribute copies of the List of Essential Requirements for Success and the Key Assumptions List. Distribute two copies of the Key Assumptions Options for each Choice.
- Ask Team members to mark their recommended Key Assumption on the list of Key Assumption Options for each Choice without putting their name on the page.
- Post total votes for each Key Assumption Option for each Choice.
- Beginning with the first Choice, ask members for the reasons for their Key Assumption recommendations, and post keywords. Repeat for each Choice and its Key Assumptions.
- Ask for observations of themes and patterns in the recommendations. Keywords.
- Vote again on the Key Assumptions Options for each Choice. The results go into the Decision Book as recommendations from the Team.

Exercise Work Product

- Key Assumptions—Team recommendations

A photo or modestly elaborated recording of the Team's whiteboard notes will go in the Team Meeting Notes section of the Decision Book. Create cleaned-up and stand-alone versions of the Key Assumptions Recommendations and file them in the Team Meeting Notes section. The Recommendations will also go in the Decisions to Be Made section.

Exercise 12-4, "Choosing the Future—Team Recommendations," asks the Team for its recommendations for the decisions facing the Decision Makers when they choose the future path for the organization. The Decision to be made could be a simple Yes-or-No choice—go forward with an initiative or not. Or there could be a complex Decision Tree network and multiple Future Choice options.

This exercise ranks the Choices for the Future rather than selecting the final go-forward Choice. The Decision Makers are not asking the Team to tell them which Future Choice to select. The ranking will give the Deciders insight into how the Team evaluates and balances the Choices against each other. The Deciders will learn from how the Team weighs the pluses, minuses, and risks of the Choices when weighed against each other.

Adapt this exercise's format to the complexity of the decisions on the table. If the Team is only Decision Makers, skip this exercise.

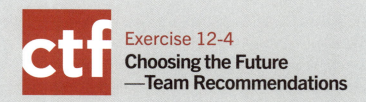

Exercise 12-4
Choosing the Future —Team Recommendations

In this exercise, the Team gives its recommendations to the Deciders by ranking the Future Choices.

Exercise Steps

- Distribute a list of the Choices for the Future, the Benefits and Barriers Matrix, and the SRV Profiles. Also, distribute the Decision Agenda and two copies of the List of Essential Decisions.
- For each Decision, ask Team members to rank the decision options on the List of Essential Decisions (first, second, third, etc., or Yes/No) without putting their name on the List.
- Post ranking totals for each Decision.
- Beginning with the first Decision, ask members to describe the reasons for their ranking, and post keywords. Repeat for each Decision.
- Ask for observations of themes and patterns in the rankings. Keywords.
- Ask for agreement to eliminate the lowest-ranking one or two options for each Decision or list of Choices.
- Re-rank the remaining high-ranking options for each Decision. The results go into the Decision Book as recommendations from the Team.

Exercise Work Product

- Choices for the Future—Team Rankings

A photo or modestly elaborated recording of the Team's whiteboard notes will go in the Team Meeting Notes section of the Decision Book. Create cleaned-up and stand-alone versions of the Future Choices Recommendations and file them in the Team Meeting Notes section. The Recommendations will also go in the Decisions to Be Made section.

CTF TEAM REPORT—DECISION BOOK AND DECISION PACKAGE

The Team's work is to prepare the Decision Makers to make the best decisions possible with the information available. The Team does its work as the consultant/advisor to the Decision Makers whether the Team is a CEO and four senior staff or a board of directors with no outside members. Advising and Deciding are distinctly different in their processes and their goals. The Team, including Deciders, does the creative work, develops options, and evaluates barriers. The Decider or Deciders are charged with choosing the organization's path forward.

If you are the CEO, company owner, or board member who will make the final decisions on the direction of the organization, work hard to keep an open and questioning mind and stay creative while participating in the Team's Advising exercises. Determination, realism, and clarity should drive your Deciding work.

The Team prepares two reports for the Decision Makers—the Decision Book and the Decision Package.

Capture What You Create—The Decision Book

The Decision Book is a chronological record of exercise work products, Team meeting notes, and background information. The Decision Book

---

If you are the CEO, company owner, or board member who will make the final decisions on the direction of the organization, work hard to keep an open and questioning mind and stay creative while participating in the Team's Advising exercises.

captures the Team's work and is a resource for the Team and for the Decision Makers during their decision-making process. The Team Leader or facilitator compiles the Team exercise work products and puts them in the Decision Book. The Decision Book is a three-ring, loose-leaf workbook or Google Docs folder.

The Book will have sections such as these.

DECISION BOOK OUTLINE
1. Challenges—Issues to Be Addressed
2. Goals
3. Background Information
4. Team Meeting Notes
5. Choices for the Future
6. Key Assumptions
7. Decisions to Be Made

After Team meetings, the Team Leader takes pictures of the whiteboard or flip charts. Copies of the photos or modestly elaborated versions of the whiteboard notes are posted in the Team Meeting Notes section of the Decision Book and become a chronology of meetings results and work products.

Good practice is for the Team Leader to write a more complete version of the whiteboard notes. Often, the words or phrases on the board record an idea meaningful at the time but not understandable later. While the exercise is fresh, flesh out the notes. Elaborating the meeting notes is not intended to create a lengthy and detailed memo. The document can still look like outline meeting notes. Fill in enough to make the core ideas understandable later.

You may have developed background information as preparation for the Team's work. This information, or summaries, go in the Decision Book to make them easily accessible by the Decision Makers.

The Team will create Challenges, Goals, Choices, Key Assumptions, and Decisions "Statements" at the conclusion of the exercises. The Statements are part of the chronological Team Meeting Notes, and they are also filed in their own Decision Book sections so they can be easily found.

At the conclusion of each exercise, a good practice is for the Team Leader or facilitator to ask whether the exercise conclusions suggest adjusting the Decisions, Choices, or other topics impacting the decision-making agenda.

- ▸ Do we see the opportunity differently?
- ▸ Do we want to adjust our goals now that we better understand the threat?

If the Team's understanding of a decision topic changes, the updated Statement goes in its section of the Book. The Decision Makers can review the most current version of the Statement in its section of the Book. This process keeps the Team focused on the decisions to be made and the big picture driving the Team's work.

Agenda for Deciding—Decision Package

When the Team completes its exercises and decision-making begins, the Team Leader or facilitator will compile a Decision Package. The Decision Package pulls key information from the Decision Book and organizes it into a single file or document. The Decision Package becomes the core of the meeting agenda when the Deciders choose the future for the company.

The Decision Package identifies the topics to be discussed and the decisions to be made. The Decision Book is a backup resource. The Decision Package can include the following:

DECISION PACKAGE OUTLINE
1. Challenges—Opportunities or Threats
2. Goals for the Company and This Initiative
3. Choices
4. Key Assumptions to Make
5. Decisions to Make

In the Choices section, create a profile of each Choice, including its Benefits and Barriers Matrix and the SRV Profile. Include other summary information in the Decision Package such as the following:

- Problem Statement
- Strategic Goals Statement
- Operational Goals Statement
- Essential Requirements for Success Matrix

The Team Leader has the prime responsibility for compiling the Decision Package taking summary material from the Decision Book. Brief introductory text will be the only new material. Handle the Decision Package with the board-level confidentiality practiced in the company.

Recognize that the "company" doing CTF could be a small nonprofit or a large corporation—two guys in a conference room or a large trucking company. I have outlined the generic process for preparing the Decision Book and the Decision Package. Start with this format and simplify or expand to match your circumstances. Adapt the CTF process to your organization and your Team.

KEY TAKEAWAYS

1. The Team's work is to prepare the Decision Makers to make the best decisions possible with the information available.
2. Courage is required to ask, "Have we gotten this right?"
3. Important initiatives with big potential will succeed or falter on the unspoken preferences, hopes, and fears of those involved.
4. The Team is your advisor. Recognizing the value of their insights and deciding what to do with them are your responsibilities.
5. If you are the CEO, company owner, or board member who will make the final decisions on the direction of the organization, work hard to keep an open and questioning mind and stay creative while participating in the Team's Advising exercises.

PART 1: PREPARE THE COMPANY AND YOURSELF

PART 2: DEFINE THE CHALLENGE

PART 3: IMAGINE SUCCESS

PART 4: CREATE OPTIONS

PART 5: EVALUATE BARRIERS TO SUCCESS

PART 6: CHOOSE THE FUTURE

Chapter Topics

The Decision—Its Meaning

Decision-Making Tools

How to Choose—The Process

Choose the Future

Summing Up

CHAPTER 13

CHOOSE THE FUTURE
Decide.

You create the future by the choices you make. You and your Team have created a vision of success for the company. You have created options and evaluated barriers. You will never have perfect information. But you must choose. That is your job as the leader. When the time comes to decide, decide.

Create the Future—the CTF process—is about choosing the future. I am not guaranteeing your organization will get to the exact place you imagine. It probably will not. But you are choosing a path toward the future you want.

This chapter takes you through decision-making steps to choose, from the available options, the Future Choice best reflecting your goals, risk tolerance, and values.

This chapter's topics are:

The Decision—Its Meaning
Begin by being clear about the organization you lead and the interests you represent when choosing the future. Then describe the character of the success you hope to achieve.

Decision-Making Tools
Test votes and other decision-making tools encourage sharing and learning before you make the final decisions.

How to Choose—The Process
I outline a structured step-by-step process for choosing the future.

Choose the Future
Begin by specifying the Key Assumptions you will be making and characterizing

the Future Choices under consideration. Then select the Choice for the Future best matching your goals, risk tolerance, and values.

Summing Up
I recap what you have accomplished and what I hope you take away from this book.

If the CTF Team includes non-Decision Makers, you probably did several Chapter 12 exercises developing Team recommendations for the SRV Profiles, Key Assumptions, and perhaps the preferred Future Choice. The results of these exercises are advisory to the Decision Makers. In this chapter, the Decision Makers address the same topics, but the discussion is central to making the final decisions. The exercises also gave the Deciders an opportunity to discuss these topics in a more open forum only including other Decision Makers before making the final choices.

As I have said several times in earlier chapters, you (the Decision Maker) could be a formal board of directors or Executive Committee working with key leadership and paid outside consultants. Or, you could be a company owner, department head, or aspiring entrepreneur working with one or two colleagues. In this chapter, I keep the Decision Maker exercises in a facilitated team meeting format to make them consistent with the format of other CTF exercises. If the team meeting exercise format is right for your situation, use it. If the discrete team exercises are too complicated for your situation, pull out what is helpful for what you are trying to accomplish. Simplify and focus on what is important to you.

If you make the important decisions by yourself, use these exercises as a guide and checklist. My recommendation is that you write down your "decisions" at each exercise step—as though you are at the whiteboard. Finish the exercises and choose the go-forward Future Choice. Put your notes down and walk away for a day. If you are still OK with your decisions after thinking about them for a day, the decision is made.

In some cases, putting the options you have on an apples-to-apples comparative basis will be the most important phase of the decision-making process. In other cases, building a shared understanding of the decisions to be made and the rationale for the final decisions will be the most important part of the decision-making process. Pick one or two "exercises" most helpful for your priorities and skip the others or use them as a rough guide to the other discussions you have when making the final decisions.

You probably have established board or committee-meeting agenda formats that you use when making important decisions. Adapt these exercises to the meeting format you normally use. Use the decision-making processes and tools I outline here in your established agenda format to address your priorities for the decisions you must make.

If you are a member of the board or committee that will make the final decisions, this chapter profiles your preparation for participating in the board decision-making and steps you can take to share your views and learn from other board members before the board as a whole makes its decisions.

THE DECISION—ITS MEANING

You began CTF with three Leadership Principles:

- I will create the future by the choices I make.
- I will decide.
- I am not the company.

Keep these principles in mind as you prepare to select the organization's future path. Your responsibility is to decide—to choose. By deciding, you are creating the future. And your responsibility for the organization is separate from your responsibility for yourself.

The Create the Future work began with:

- A Challenge—an opportunity or threat
- A concept of Success

Before beginning the decision-making exercises, you have four homework assignments:

1. Identify the "company" or organization and its constituents.

2. Describe the impact of each Choice on important constituencies.
3. Characterize your "ideal" Future Choice by its Success, Risk, and Values Profile.
4. Identify differences you have with the Team or Decider consensus SRV Profiles of each Choice.

These assignments, outlined below, are "highlighted notes" for yourself and are not Team exercises.

The Company and Its Constituents

Decision Makers act for the benefit of "the company." The company could be a division of a larger company or a corporation with many shareholders. Your "company" could be a nonprofit agency or government department. The decision you are making might be whether to launch an experimental new product. Your department or small company will be impacted by the results of the experiment but no one else. Or you could be the CEO of Boeing asked to choose the level of safety inspections on new aircraft before they go into service.

Before choosing the company's future, outline your concept of "the company." What organization are you representing when you make the decisions? With the "company" profiled, identify the interests and constituents that may be impacted by the choices you are about to make. Shareholders are a constituency if the "company" is a corporation. Who else will be materially impacted by the Choices under consideration?

If the Decision Makers are the board of directors of a corporation, their fiduciary obligation is to act in the best interests of the shareholders—all shareholders. "The best interests of the shareholders" is an ambiguous standard. Some shareholders want long-term value creation, and others want cash on the barrelhead tomorrow. Even if you are the only shareholder, "for the benefit of the shareholders" is not an explicit criterion for making decisions.

Keeping staff committed to their work is an important leadership goal for the welfare of all organizations. Keeping customers satisfied is a requirement for the long-term viability of all companies. The impact of decisions on the local community may be a consideration. Profile the major constituents and their interests in the organization.

Impact on the Constituents

Sketch out your assessment of how each Choice will impact the company, its shareholders, and the company's constituents. Focus on the differences between the Choices and the qualitative impacts—the "meaning of the Choices" to the constituents. Share your impact expectations with other Deciders by doing Exercise 13-2, "Characterize the Choices for the Future."

Success, Risk, and Values—Your Preferences

A board member, advisor, or spouse might ask, "What are you trying to accomplish with this decision? What is the meaning of this decision?" The choices could be:

- Save the company or give up on it.
- Put new family leadership in charge or move to professional management.
- Choose one new product from several with growth potential while not putting the company at risk.
- Stand pat or launch a project with a high failure risk.
- Start a new company or keep the big company job.

You have a vision of success for the company, an assessment of the company's capabilities, and an understanding of the risk/reward profile of the Choices available. Your preferred Choice will be the combination of Success, Risk, and Values you believe is most appropriate for the company where it is today. The Future Choice you select from among the available options will be in the Venn diagram space where your goals are achieved at an acceptable risk and your values are expressed.

What is the meaning of this decision?

The Meaning of Your Choice: Goals, Risks, and Values

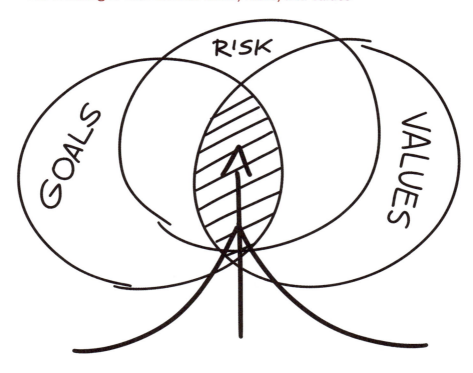

Ideally, each Future Choice will have a big payoff and no risk. Few Choices will have that profile. With the challenge before you and the concept of success in mind, step back from the Future Choices on the table and profile the combination of Success, Risk, and Values you ideally hope to achieve when selecting the Future Choice. What would an "ideal Future Choice" look like? You want the selected Future Choice to achieve "Success," but the Choice selected should also reflect your risk tolerance and your values. Are you making a "go big or go home" decision or a low-margin/low-risk decision? What combination of Success, Risk, and Values do you hope to find in the selected Future Choice?

None of the Choices available are likely to match your ideal SRV Profile, but you will have set a standard for evaluating the Choices.

Your Differences with the Team SRV Profiles

The Team or the Deciders themselves prepared an SRV Profile of each Choice as

Strong leaders will have optimism, determination, and generosity as core values when making decisions.

---

part of the Prepare to Choose work of Chapter 12. If you are the Decision Maker or a member of the board or committee that will make the final decisions, review the Team/Decider consensus Profiles and note your differences with these assessments. If the profiles closely match your assessment, go with them. If your assessment is different in some cases, make marginal notes on a copy of the profiles. The SRV Profiles and the Benefits and Barriers Matrix are the primary summary comparisons you will use when selecting your preferred Future Choice.

These notes should not go in the Decision Book. Use your notes to guide your thinking when making the final decisions or your contributions to the decision-making discussion.

The Right and Wrong Decision

Strong leaders will have optimism, determination, and generosity as core values when making decisions. A wrong decision would be based on fear, greed, envy, laziness, anger, maliciousness, smugness, or arrogance. Avoiding a decision is the wrong decision.

Decisions you make are an expression of your values and who you are. Put yourself in a place and frame of mind where the values expressed by your decisions—strength and optimism—are values you want to represent you.

> *The only person you are destined to become is the person you decide to be.* —Ralph Waldo Emerson

Future Choice options surviving the CTF process will not be "right" or "wrong" choices. When you select one option over another, you will be choosing a goals preference, a risk preference, and a values preference.

DECISION-MAKING TOOLS

When the Decision Makers are a board or committee—more than one person—the following tools help draw on the experience and wisdom of all members.

Reveal Assumptions: Verbalize Key Assumptions and outline member's assessment of the Success, Risk, and Values Profiles to reveal the members' underlying assumptions and judgments about the Choices being considered. Encourage each Decider to talk about what is important to them, what they assume will happen, and their characterization of the Choices.

Take Test Votes: Take test votes and encourage members to talk about why they voted the way they did. Have the members share their rationale for their test votes. Vote again and be clear that changing your vote is OK.

Rank Options: Before a final vote, rank the options and discuss the rankings. Have members share their ranking of the Choices with other members. Drop low-ranking Choices and rank again.

Look for Themes and Clarify Differences: Find areas of agreement. Surface the reasons for differences.

Reveal the Strength of Preferences: Ask for the strength of member preferences. Members with weak or no preferences may be open to concurring with an option other members strongly prefer.

Respect: Acknowledge and respect each Decider's views and decisions.

These techniques build transparency, sharing, and learning into your decision-making. At the end of the decision-making meeting, you want every participant to feel they were heard and, if possible, to accept the results even if the selected Choice is not their preference.

If you will make the final decisions by yourself, use these tools to structure your thinking when choosing one option over another.

HOW TO CHOOSE—THE PROCESS

Before you and other Decision Makers decide the organization's future direction, agree on how you will make final decisions—majority vote, consensus, or CEO/Chair decision.

You probably have established protocols for how the leader or board makes decisions. If you do not have an established procedure, work through how you will select the preferred Future Choice before putting the question on the table. Avoid mixing debate about where to take the company with debate about deciding who can make the decision. Finalize "who will decide?" before tackling "where are we going?"

Your process for making the decision will impact the quality of the decision. Begin by being explicit about your assumptions when selecting the Future Choice, whether you are an individual Decision Maker or a member of the board or committee. Then share with other Deciders your characterization of the Future Choices. Rank the Choices and cast test votes before making the final selections. These steps encourage you and others to share your views and learn from each other. You do not want someone, after the meeting, to say, "I wish you had told me how you were thinking!"

How you decide will also send a message to others involved and impacted. You may influence the execution of the decision by building or losing support among those who will execute the plan.

Agenda for Choosing the Future

Whether the Decision Maker is a board, a committee, or just you, the decision-making agenda should include the following.

Seven Decision Steps

1. Decisions—*Review the Decision Agenda. Finalize the description of the decisions to be made.*
2. Choices—*Review the Choices for the Future. Considering everything you have learned, finalize the Choices.*
3. Key Assumptions—*Identify Key Assumptions. Be clear what assumptions you are making.*
4. Ideal Success, Risk, and Values Profile—*Describe your "ideal" Future*

Choice by its Success, Risk, and Values Profile. Describe what the best outcome would look like.
5. SRV Profile for each Choice—*Describe each Choice using the SRV Profile format. Clarify the differences between the options.*
6. The Company and its Constituencies—*Identify the shareholders and other constituents most impacted by the Choices. Characterize the impact of the Choices on them.*
7. Choose—*Choose the future path for the company.*

Key Decision Steps

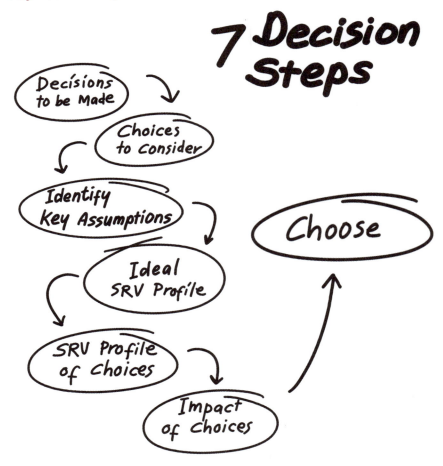

Prepare Yourself

Ask yourself, "Am I ready to choose?" Some level of apprehension is natural. You are making decisions on behalf of your investors, your leadership team, your customers, your employees, your lenders, your community, and yourself.

Your frame of mind will impact the quality of your decisions. Prepare yourself. When I must make an important decision, I get on my sailboat, go to the beach, or listen to classical music. I get away from distractions. American football quarterback Tom Brady put on headphones and listed to music like "Yes Indeed" by rappers Drake and Lil Baby before a game. Walking, meditating, doing yoga, taking a run, or talking with a trusted advisor could be your way of working through a complex topic and preparing to decide.

When making an important decision, let your Slow Mind do its work.

- Find a way to remove your ego from the process.
- Be clear about what you are trying to accomplish.
- Give yourself time to pull your thoughts together.
- Get in a positive and confident frame of mind.
- Listen, learn, judge, and decide.
- Be comfortable choosing and moving on.

Center yourself with these two ideas:

- You are not the company.
- You will decide on behalf of the company.

The Team Might Be Wrong!

Team members worked hard to develop information, insights, and options that would not be available without their contributions. As you begin your decision-making work, keep the Team's work in an appropriate context. Even when the Team includes only Decision Makers, the Team did the creative work as an advisor to the Decision Makers. The Team did not select the future path for the company. Advising is a different mindset than deciding.

A major Chicago corporation engaged me to evaluate a business sector they

Your judgment is your contribution to the process of choosing your company's future.

were considering entering. My case team looked at the economics of the business sector, its history, and its future prospects. We examined the underlying technology and where the technology was going. We profiled companies in the business. For the final report, we recommended a strategy for entering the business.

A year later, I met with the client during a trip to Chicago. On the plane, I reread our recommendations. After a catching-up conversation, I asked if they had adopted our top recommendation. No, they had not. I then asked if they had adopted our second recommendation. No, they did not go with that one either. Feeling a little embarrassed, I said I was sorry our work had not been more helpful.

On the contrary, the client said our work was extremely helpful to them. They had not asked us to match the company's current capabilities and plans to the requirements for entering the new business. They had taken our work and redid the analysis using our approach to the business opportunity, the information we gathered, and their existing capabilities. A different entry strategy emerged.

Our advisory work's value was teaching the client how to do the analysis and how to formulate a plan to enter the business—not the specific recommendations.

You are the Decider. You will choose the company's future with the Team's work as a resource to be considered. From what you have learned and your experience and judgment, should the Decision Agenda or the Choices prepared by the Team be adjusted? Could they be phrased more clearly? Be sure you are solving the right problem before choosing the solution. The Team's recommendations are what they are—recommendations. Your judgment is your contribution to the process of choosing the company's future.

CHOOSE THE FUTURE

The Team has done its work. Your work as a Decision Maker begins. You will make Key Assumptions, describe your ideal SRV Profile, evaluate the options available, and select a Future Choice. The decisions you make will determine the future of your organization.

Your Message

As the leader of a decision-making group, your message to other Deciders should be:

- We are now choosing the future of our "company."
- What we decide is important to the company and to everyone involved.
- What is said in this room today stays in this room.
- "Speak now or forever hold your peace."
- Respect each other's views and opinions.
- Use our best judgment when making these important decisions.
- Together we will choose our company's future.

Respect for the process you are undertaking, combined with a determination to choose, is the message.

Choosing the Path to the Future

There is no "Create the Future answer" to your company's challenge. *Create the Future* is about how to decide and not what to decide. Employing CTF tools, you and other Decision Makers will consider the available information, apply your judgment, and decide.

After selecting the go-forward Future Choice, execution barriers, competitors, and other external factors will directly challenge what you are trying to accomplish. The company's response to these execution challenges will determine the Future Choice's success or failure. As the Decision Maker,

---

As the Decision Maker, you are not choosing the future. You are choosing the path to the future. The company will create the future by each step it takes along that path.

you are not choosing the future. You are choosing the path to the future. The company will create the future by each step it takes along that path.

Decision Maker Exercises

The exercises in this chapter take you through the Seven Decision Steps for selecting the Future Choice. The exercises are in the form of a "facilitated whiteboard meeting" for a board or committee. If you and one or two others are using the exercises, adapt them to your situation. The exercises can also be used as agenda segments for the decision-making meeting. The exercise structure and the questions asked will impose a helpful discipline on your process.

> **Exercise 13-1** KEY ASSUMPTIONS BY DECISION MAKERS
> **Exercise 13-2** CHARACTERIZE THE CHOICES FOR THE FUTURE
> **Exercise 13-3** CHOOSE THE FUTURE

These exercises assume the group has a "leader" or facilitator who is asking the group questions. Asking the leader or facilitator of the Team exercises to lead the Decision Makers' meeting is an option. If the group has three or more members, designate who will lead the meeting if it is not the board chair or facilitator.

Let's get started by specifying the assumptions you are making when you select your preferred Future Choice. The Team identified Key Assumptions influencing the success potential of each Future Choice and identified Key Assumption Options. Exercise 13-1, "Key Assumptions by Decision Makers," guides you to specify the assumptions you will use when selecting the preferred Future Choice.

This exercise encourages you and other Deciders to be clear with yourself and other Deciders about what assumptions you are making. You reveal your preferences and share your reasoning. The exercise calls for "distributing" copies of earlier exercise work products. If the Decision Package follows the meeting agenda, the exercise work products are clustered in the Package with the relevant agenda decision to be made.

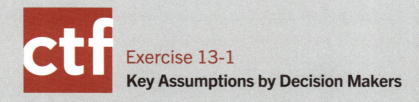

Exercise 13-1
Key Assumptions by Decision Makers

In this exercise, Decision Makers specify the assumptions they are making about the outcomes of uncertain events that could materially impact the success of the Choices for the Future. Decision Makers finalize the Decision Agenda and the description of the Future Choices.

Exercise Steps

- Distribute copies of the Decision Agenda. Ask for comments and suggested revisions to the Decision Tree and the description of the Decisions to Be Made. By vote or another process for making "decisions," finalize the Decision Agenda.
- Distribute the Choices for the Future. Ask for suggested revisions to the description of the Choices. By vote, finalize the description/specification of the Choices for the Future.
- Distribute the Key Assumptions List, two copies of the Key Assumptions Options, and the Team recommendations for the Assumptions, if made. Ask members to mark their preferred Key Assumptions for each Choice. Total the results.
- Beginning with the first Choice and its Assumptions, ask members to describe the reasons for their vote. Post keywords. Repeat for each Choice's Assumption Options.
- Ask for observations and themes in the Assumption preferences.
- Vote on the Key Assumptions again. A consensus would be desirable but is not a requirement. The second-vote results go into the meeting minutes, if appropriate.

Exercise Work Products

- Decision Agenda—Final Version
- Choices for the Future—Final Description
- Key Assumptions—Decision Maker Assumptions

You probably have established practices for recording meeting minutes, member votes, and decisions. That procedure should be followed for the results of this exercise and Exercise 13-3, "Choose the Future." You can preserve the exercise results in the Decision Book, but handling them as "board minutes" will give them a higher level of confidentiality protection. Legal counsel to the board may recommend limiting what is recorded in the meeting minutes prior to recording the final decisions.

After identifying the Key Assumptions you and the other Deciders are using, do Exercise 13-2, "Characterize the Choices for the Future." This exercise includes four elements where the Deciders:

- Describe their "ideal" SRV Profile of a Future Choice
- Characterize each Choice by its SRV Profile
- Identify the company's most important constituencies and describe the impact of the Choices on these constituencies
- Profile the Decision Makers' motivations for selecting one Choice over another and their perception of each Choice's primary characteristics

Having this discussion before selecting the preferred the Future Choice is an opportunity for Deciders to learn from each other, clarify their own thinking, and adjust their thinking before making the final decisions.

It is not hard to make decisions
when you know what your values are.
—Attributed to Roy Disney

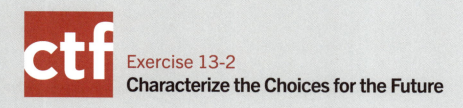

Exercise 13-2
Characterize the Choices for the Future

This exercise asks Decision Makers to characterize their "ideal" Future Choice and the Choices under consideration. Deciders describe the impact of the Choices on important company constituencies. This exercise is an opportunity for Decision Makers to share their thinking and learn from others before selecting the Future Choice.

Exercise Steps

▸ Distribute the Decision Agenda and the Choices for the Future. Distribute the Benefits and Barriers Matrix, the Success, Risk, and Values Profiles for each Choice, and other summary information relevant to the final Choice selections.

▸ Outline an SRV Profile on the whiteboard. Ask members what characteristics they believe the Future Choice should have. Post keywords within the Profile format. Ask why these characteristics are important.

▸ Outline a table with Choices listed in the left column. SRV Profile and Advantages/Disadvantages are the other column headings. Referencing the Team or Decider consensus SRV Profile of each Choice, ask members whether they agree with the characterizations or if they would characterize the Choices differently.

▸ Ask members what they believe are the primary advantages and disadvantages of each Choice.

▸ Outline a three-column table listing Choices in the left column. Constituents and Impacts head the other columns. Beginning with Shareholders, list the organization's constituents likely to be materially impacted by each Future Choice. Ask members to describe the impacts of each Choice on the constituents.

▸ On a new section of the board, ask Deciders what the primary drivers of their Future Choice selection are.

Exercise Work Products

1. Decision Maker characterization of their "ideal" Future Choice SRV Profile and of the Future Choices under consideration
2. Decision Maker assessment of the impact the Choices will have on important constituents
3. Primary drivers of the Decision Makers' selection of a Future Choice

The results should not go in the Decision Book and probably should not go in the official meeting minutes. The exercise is primarily an education and sharing exercise and a dry run for the following decision-making exercise. A photograph of the meeting notes can be included in an informal record of the meeting if approved by the company's legal counsel.

Characterizing the Choices, Raise Revenues

characterize the choices

What do we want?
- Success — Fin. stability, Rev. ↑, Higher profit
- Risk — some-not much, Not much change
- Values — Lean & mean, purposeful

(Sell Co.)

Choices	Team SRV profile ??	Advantage + Disadvantage
Ⓐ New products	Harder to do. Expect cust. accept.	Know cust. Have tech + Distribution
Ⓑ More sales & marketing $	Too easy A solution. What then? May not work	Not long term solution. Costly
Ⓒ New cust. categories	Hard to do. Now sales team? Should try/exp.	High risk. Long term opportunity. Not clear what they will buy

The Challenge could be "We are a leading producer of disposable baby diapers, and we are losing market share. How do we sell more diapers?" Or "We invented instant photography and own the market. Should we develop digital cameras and compete with our film products?"

The leaders of Pampers and Polaroid faced the same challenges every business, nonprofit, and public agency faces. Competition, technology, customer preferences, and the economic and financial environment change constantly. To succeed, even to survive, your organization must adapt. Considering all ideas as good ideas is the place to start. In the end, you must choose which of the good ideas is the right path forward for your company, starting from where it stands today.

The Polaroid and Pampers leaders had essentially unlimited access to talented staff, deeply experienced consultants, and funding. Eventually, the leaders came to a point where they had to choose the future path for their company.

Pampers set up a CTF-like process for learning from mothers what they wanted from a diaper and then changed the product. And Pampers changed how their diapers' value was presented to customer moms. Polaroid invested heavily in developing digital photography but would not bring the technology to the market where it would compete with its film products. Pampers regained market leadership, and Polaroid went into bankruptcy.

The time to choose has come. You know as much as you will know about the challenge facing the company and your options. Your job is to choose. Exercise 13-3, "Choose the Future," is your guide.

You and other Decision Makers have shared your views on the Choices and heard other viewpoints. You can simply vote and select which Choice to pursue. If most Deciders highly favor one Choice, that may be the best next step.

Henry Fonda's movie from 1957, *12 Angry Men*, comes to mind. Eleven members of the jury are convinced the inner-city teen is guilty. Fonda's character thought the defendant might be guilty but was not sure. The movie portrays the drama of Fonda's questions in the jury room. Other jurors want to vote quickly and leave the hot, sweaty room. Fonda's patient and persistent questions about what the evidence demonstrates eventually convinces one juror and then another and another that the defendant is innocent.

As a Decision Maker, your job is to make difficult decisions. You are making these decisions drawing on your experience and your judgment. Even if you believe the best option is clear, investing a little extra time in testing your approach is usually a smart move. When we make important decisions by ourselves, without the advice and counsel of trusted advisors, we hear only the advice and counsel of our own voice. Take time to understand other points of view and test your assessments before you make a final decision. Being open to learning from the experiences and views of others reduces the risk of making a big mistake.

Adapt the exercise steps profiled here to the decisions you must make and to the history and composition of the decision-making committee or board. Simplify the process for two or three deciders. At the end of the meeting, decide what will be communicated about the decisions, if anything, to Team members, company staff, and those outside the company. Decide who will be the communicator and what they will communicate about the decisions made.

Notes from this Decision Makers' meeting will be valuable as a history of the CTF work and a foundation for future planning and decision-making. Ask corporate counsel how many of the Decision Maker meeting notes to save and what should be destroyed. The results could be saved in the Decision Book, but handling them as "board minutes" will give them a higher level of confidentiality protection. Generally, board meeting minutes are minimal. Planning documents such as the Decision Book involving non-board members are probably safe to preserve. But the best approach is to ask corporate counsel what is safe to keep.

Exercise 13-3
Choose the Future

In this exercise, you and other Decision Makers select the preferred Future Choice and the company's path forward.

Exercise Steps

- Distribute the Choices for the Future list. Distribute the Decision Agenda, including the Decision Tree and two lists of Decisions to Be Made. If the Team ranked the Choices, distribute the ranking.
- For each Decision, ask Deciders to rank the options or Choices (first, second, etc., or Yes/No). (Adapt this process to the Decision list and the Decision Tree.)
- Total the first, second etc. rankings and Yes-and-No votes for each decision.
- Beginning with the first Decision, ask for reasons for the rankings. Post the reasons on the whiteboard (key words). Repeat for each Decision on the Decision Tree. Do not associate reasons with individual members.
- Ask for observations and themes.
- Ask for agreement to eliminate the lowest-ranking branches from the Decision Tree or the lowest-ranking Choices. The goal is to identify the two or three decision paths or Choices with the strongest support. With a simplified Decision Tree or shortened list of Choices, ask for a second round of ranking.
- With the second round of rank voting posted, ask how strongly members feel about their preferences.
- From the remaining decisions on the Decision Tree and the Choices still under consideration, ask the Decision Makers to make each Decision in the sequence of decisions on the Decision Tree and to select the preferred Future Choice.

> The decision process will follow the Decision Agenda format and may include a sequence of Decisions to be recorded in the meeting minutes. Follow established practice for taking votes or reaching consensus and for recording or not recording member votes.

Exercise Work Product
> Choice for the Future—Decision Maker selection

SUMMING UP

Your Guiding Principles

Most of our time every day is spent dealing with the details of that day. We seldom step back and ask ourselves what we want to accomplish next month, next year, or five years from now. Through this book, I hope you see that every day you are creating the future for your organization and yourself. You create the future:

By the choices you make
By the decisions you make

A starting point for all important decisions is understanding who you are. Finding your Zone of Leadership is a good place to start. You are not the company. The company will be more successful, and you will be more successful when you are in your Zone of Leadership.

Going forward, when you face an important challenge, I hope you

---

Every day you are creating the future for your organization and yourself.

will slow down and engage your Slow Mind. Approach each important decision with:

> A concept of success
> A measure of your risk tolerance
> An understanding of your values

Strive to create a future for your company, expressing your vision of success, your risk tolerance, and your values.

Your Accomplishment

You began with a Challenge—an opportunity or a threat. Using the Create the Future process, you, other Decision Makers, and the entire Team have:

> Characterized the opportunity or threat
> Defined success
> Established goals
> Created choices
> Evaluated barriers and risks
> Identified Key Assumptions to be made
> Characterized the Choices
> Identified the Key Assumptions you are making

And finally, you have

> Decided—made a choice

You have chosen the future path for your organization.

Create the Future

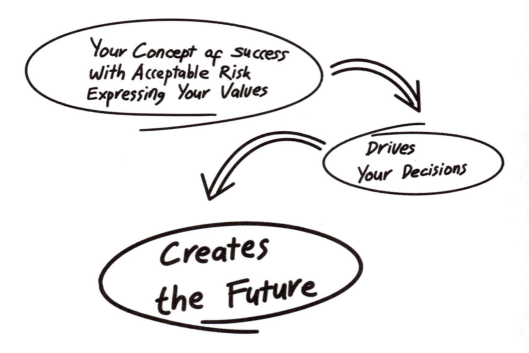

Thank your fellow Decision Makers and Team members for their investment in the future of the company and acknowledge what they have accomplished.

The decisions you have made will create your company's future. Now begins the hard work of executing on your decisions.

Now begins the hard work of executing your decisions.

KEY TAKEAWAYS

1. Strong leaders will have optimism, determination, and generosity as core values when making decisions.
2. A wrong decision would be based on fear, greed, envy, laziness, anger, maliciousness, smugness, or arrogance.
3. As the Decision Maker, you are not choosing the future. You are choosing the path to the future. The company will create the future by each step it takes along that path.
4. Your judgment is your contribution to the process of choosing the company's future.
5. The decisions you make are an expression of your values. Put yourself in a place and frame of mind where the values expressed by your decisions—strength and optimism—are values you want to represent you.
6. Be comfortable choosing and moving on.

- PART 1: PREPARE THE COMPANY AND YOURSELF
- PART 2: DEFINE THE CHALLENGE
- PART 3: IMAGINE SUCCESS
- PART 4: CREATE OPTIONS
- PART 5: EVALUATE BARRIERS TO SUCCESS
- **PART 6: CHOOSE THE FUTURE**

Chapter Topics

Create a Vision Statement

Develop an Execution Plan

Lead the Implementation

CHAPTER 14

IMPLEMENTATION
Make it happen.

Execution creates the most value.

Whether you developed a new software platform in your dorm room to be known as Windows or have announced to the world that you will land a man on the moon and have a multibillion-dollar budget, plans are just plans. Execution is where your plan becomes a reality and where the most value is created.

This book is about choosing which future path to pursue. Execution along the path you have chosen creates the future. Because execution is so important, I will end by highlighting important steps you can take to maximize the probability that you will realize the future you imagine.

You have decided which Choice for the Future to pursue. As the leader, your next assignment and the topics of this chapter are:

Create a Vision Statement
Compose a compelling Vision Statement.

Develop an Execution Plan
Create a realistic plan for the company and its leadership reflecting the approved risk level and anticipating the primary execution barriers.

Lead the Implementation
Take leadership of the execution plan by anticipating the primary barriers to success, learning from failure, and acknowledging the cultural barriers to your execution plan.

CREATE A VISION STATEMENT
You have completed a complex process, ending with selecting the

Execution is where your plan becomes a reality and where the most value is created.

---

organization's future path. You have chosen a vision of the future and a rationale for that vision, expressing where the organization is today and where it will go tomorrow. The last step of your last exercise, "Choose the Future," was deciding what to tell your organization and the outside world about the Team's work, the decisions made, and who should tell the story.

Your job is to compose a vision statement that will motivate your organization and the collaborators and partners required for success. If active support and participation is required by your staff, funders, suppliers, customers, and other partners, they need to know the vision and their role in your organization's path forward.

In most cases, you will communicate the decisions and the future vision for the company to your staff and others. The board of directors or executive committee may be the Decision Maker, but the CEO or executive director should be the spokesperson who communicates the decisions. There will be different audiences requiring different messages, and you must keep some information confidential. You may want to engage professional help crafting these messages.

DEVELOP AN EXECUTION PLAN

Developing an execution plan is an art in itself. Develop an execution plan with a realistic schedule and goals reflecting the level of risk you chose. Be clear to the implementation team and yourself about what your expectations are for the initiative—goals to be achieved, including leadership goals. Is the goal to grind down costs wherever you can? Or is the goal to try a high-risk experiment and learn what is feasible and what is not? The success concepts, both for the venture and for its leadership team, will be completely different for these different paths.

The Team identified the most challenging execution barriers. Your plan will highlight those risks and define special efforts to reduce the risks and monitor progress as you work to overcome the barriers.

Your job is to compose the budget, schedule, deliverables, and a "who does what" plan for bringing the vision to reality. You may want to ask the Team to review the execution plan in draft form.

LEAD THE IMPLEMENTATION

Create the Future is a process for preparing to make choices and for making difficult decisions. The value of the CTF approach to decision-making does not end when you select the Future Choice to pursue. With implementation underway, a new decision-making phase begins.

The CTF tools—Define the Challenge, Imagine Success, Create Options, Evaluate Barriers, and Choose the Future—will be needed for the decisions you must make during the implementation work. Coach the leaders you have delegated to execute the plan using CTF tools to improve their decision-making.

New venture execution is hard to do successfully. I am drawing your attention to three leadership practices that pay big benefits.

Learn from Failure

A learning and feedback system is essential in any new initiative where the assumptions you made may not come true and failure or missteps are possible. Something will go wrong. Some elements of the execution plan will work, and some will not. Commercial airline accident rates are low because of rigid failure analysis protocols that "learn from failure." Sophisticated systems like this are possible for high-value products like commercial air flights and human drugs, but they are costly.

You want to know what is working and what is not working. To be successful, you need a feedback system in place that quickly identifies failure and learns from failure. Change direction quickly and learn from what is not working.

Something will go wrong.

Establish a Monitoring and Feedback System

The Key Assumptions exercises asked for success estimates of uncertain elements during the Future Choice's implementation. The Team also made probability estimates for actions others might take or events outside the company's control. Identifying the Most Important Execution Risks and Key Assumptions enabled Decision Makers better to understand the risks of the Choices under consideration. Identifying these uncertainties also prepares you for managing risk during the execution phase.

You have management and control systems in place for ongoing business operations. If you are executing on a new project or initiative outside normal business practices and there is significant failure risk or exposure to events outside your control, set up a progress reporting system to monitor and report on the project's primary risk exposures.

The implementation project leader can use the Decision Book to prepare the monitoring system. Tracking the Important Execution Risks and the Key Assumptions underlying the Choice selected will be part of the plan. These items will not be the only risks you are monitoring, but they should be highlighted for special attention. The monitoring system should also include an exceptions-reporting system of unexpected events or outcomes outside of expected parameters. You want to be updated on progress and to know quickly when implementation is not going as planned or when something unexpected happens.

As you roll out the new initiative, monitor the validity of the assumptions you have made. If underlying assumptions turn out not to be correct, consider the implications and adjust the execution plan. Your execution plan's monitoring and feedback system will reflect the budget available and the risks to be managed. Allocate time and resources to monitor high failure risks with potential impact on execution success. Specify who receives what reports and who is authorized to make adjustments when required.

Leadership and Culture

Your organization may have existing staff and departments that can implement the decisions you make within existing capabilities. Or perhaps you must build a new organization and form new partnerships. Identify who will have primary ownership of the vision and responsibility for its implementation. Carefully select leaders who will be responsible for executing the most critical elements of the plan and achieving the goals—both measurable and non-measurable. Match the skills of the new initiative leaders to the requirements of the initiative. Leadership skills required for a fast-moving innovative venture are completely different from those required for repositioning a large, complex organization.

What will be your role if you are the CEO or executive director who led the CTF efforts? Is continuing to be the primary leader the right implementation role for you and the venture? Or should you delegate that responsibility to someone with a better skill match or to give yourself separation from the execution process? Does your Zone of Leadership suggest the best role for you?

Your organization's culture will shape the learning and feedback process. Cultural issues are often invisible barriers and are difficult to overcome. Some organizations foster a "learning community" approach. Others are hierarchical and directive. Both types of organizations will launch new initiatives whose success will depend on learning in real time while implementation is underway. Be open and transparent about addressing cultural issues—respecting existing culture and leadership while being purposeful where change is required.

Remember, something will go wrong. The expectations and tone you set will determine how quickly you will learn about it. Saying something is not working takes courage. To foster courage, you must be clear—by what you say and how you act—that you expect and welcome both good news and bad news. If you don't, you may be one of the last people to know something has gone wrong.

During the Future Choice implementation, keep the ask-and-discover

---

Success requires a continuous Create the Future Thinking cycle where you Ask, Discover, Learn, and Decide.

process going: "What have we learned? And what adjustments and new decisions must we make?"

Ultimately, success requires a continuous Create the Future Thinking cycle where you Ask, Discover, Learn, and Decide.

Create the Future Thinking Cycle

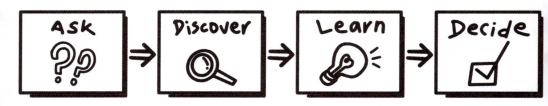

KEY TAKEAWAYS

1. Execution is where your plan becomes a reality and where the most value is created.
2. Something will go wrong.
3. You must be clear—by what you say and how you act—that you expect and welcome both good news and bad news.
4. Success requires a continuous Create the Future Thinking cycle where you Ask, Discover, Learn, and Decide.

APPENDIX A

CHAPTER KEY TAKEAWAYS

GETTING STARTED

Is this book for you? How to create the future. Chapter summaries.

- The Create the Future process is a structured methodology for defining the problem, clarifying success, developing realistic options, evaluating barriers to achieving success, and making decisions without a big consulting-firm price tag.
- Believing you can and will create the future is the foundational belief of impactful leadership.
- *Create the Future* is about how to decide, not what to decide. Choosing the future is your responsibility.
- You are not the company. Your duties to the company and to yourself are separate and different.

PART ONE: PREPARE THE COMPANY AND YOURSELF

1. **Create the Future Thinking**

   Ask, discover, learn, and decide.

   - Create the Future Thinking is an ask-questions, discover-what-you-know, and learn-from-what-you-discover process for making important decisions.
   - Your job is to ask the right questions.
   - Questioning is the path to discovery and learning.
   - All ideas are good ideas.
   - Discovering what you know and what you do not know is fundamental to smart decision-making.
   - Keep asking, "What are we learning?"
   - Ask, "What don't we know that will change our future?"

2. **Your Zone of Leadership**

   You are not the company. Choose your own future.
   - You are not the company.
   - Knowing yourself is essential to being an effective leader.
   - Your Zone of Leadership is where your passions and personal strengths overlap.
   - When you are in a job that is a good match with your Strengths and Passions, you are the right person for the job, and the job is right for you.

3. **The Leader's Role**

   Decision Maker, Leader of the Company, and Team Leader.
   - Before asking someone to help you choose a future path for the company, ask yourself, "Why should they care?"
   - Successful leaders are both decisive and vulnerable. They are open to hearing other points of view and are prepared to make decisions.
   - Get the most value from the CTF process by building on your style as a leader.

4. **Engage the Team**

   Decision Makers and trusted advisors create the future together.
   - Forming a CTF Team will help you make better decisions.
   - The personal qualities of the Team members are as important, perhaps more important, than the content of their résumé.
   - Usually, you don't need more creative people in the room. But being creative in the room must be OK.
   - Make CTF fast and fun. Don't make it complicated or a long chore.

PART TWO: DEFINE THE CHALLENGE

5. **Define the Challenge**

   Solve the right problem.
   - Defining the challenge is the first step to finding a solution.
   - Engage the Team to define the problem before asking them to solve it.
   - As the company's leader, clearly defining the challenge facing the company is your responsibility. Expressing the challenge in a way that motivates others to address it is also your responsibility.

- Be clear to the Team that you are open to their views and contributions.

PART THREE: IMAGINE SUCCESS

6. **Success, Goals, and Values**

    What success looks like.

    - Before designing your organization's one-year, two-year, or five-year plan, you need a concept of success.
    - The impactful leader changes uncertainty into hope and possibility.
    - Success is a choice.
    - Without a concept of success, all plans will be successful.
    - Keep it simple. Make the goal easy to understand and translate it into an implementation plan.

PART FOUR: CREATE OPTIONS

7. **Paths to Success**

    Different ways to solve the problem.

    - Before proposing specific initiatives your organization could pursue, ask what categories of options you have for achieving success and reaching your goals.
    - Successfully competing means the company has a successful strategy. Making a profit means the company has a viable business model.
    - The Future Choices you evaluate and the final Choice you select as the path forward for the company should express the strategy and the business model you are currently pursuing or intend to implement.

8. **Choices for the Future**

    Create options for the path to success.

    - Even if you believe you know the best initiative for addressing the company's challenge, pause and allow for the possibility that other options are worth considering.
    - Encourage unbounded and unconventional "all ideas are good ideas" thinking.
    - Don't ask for "great ideas." Start with lots of ideas, and then find the great ideas on the whiteboard.
    - *Create the Future* combines "all ideas are good ideas" creativity with disciplined reality.

PART FIVE: EVALUATE BARRIERS TO SUCCESS

9. Execution Barriers

Getting there from here.

- ▶ The future you imagine for your company might be well thought out and achievable by some company. The question is whether it is achievable by your company with its capabilities today.
- ▶ Culture will trump strategy every time.
- ▶ Growing larger by doing more of what you are already doing usually does not work.
- ▶ Leaders who make important decisions for their company while assuming someone else will figure out how to "make it work" are neglecting half their job.
- ▶ Understanding risk is the objective. Avoiding risk is not the objective.

10. Key Assumptions

What you assume will happen and will not happen.

- ▶ Underlying your choices are assumptions about what you will accomplish, what others will do, and how the world will change.
- ▶ An assumption is a prediction of an uncertain future event.
- ▶ An assumption is a choice.
- ▶ The best way to manage the risk in the assumptions you make is to be clear with yourself and your colleagues that you are making an assumption and to characterize the assumption's quality.

PART SIX: CHOOSE THE FUTURE

11. Decision Agenda

What decisions must I make?

- ▶ Making a decision—a simple concept but a complex event.
- ▶ As the leader, your job is to make decisions—to make choices.
- ▶ Engage the Team to help you be clear what decisions you must make.
- ▶ Successful leaders see decision-making as a process. Their job is to manage the process as well as make decisions.

12. **Prepare to Choose**

    Understand the "meaning" of your decision.

    ▶ The Team's work is to prepare the Decision Makers to make the best decisions possible with the information available.

    ▶ Courage is required to ask, "Have we gotten this right?"

    ▶ Important initiatives with big potential will succeed or falter on the unspoken preferences, hopes, and fears of those involved.

    ▶ The Team is your advisor. Recognizing the value of their insights and deciding what to do with them are your responsibilities.

    ▶ If you are the CEO, company owner, or board member who will make the final decisions on the direction of the organization, work hard to keep an open and questioning mind and stay creative while participating in the Team exercises.

13. **Choose the Future**

    Decide.

    ▶ Strong leaders will have optimism, determination, and generosity as core values when making decisions.

    ▶ A wrong decision would be based on fear, greed, envy, laziness, anger, maliciousness, smugness, or arrogance.

    ▶ As the Decision Maker, you are not choosing the future. You are choosing the path to the future. The company will create the future by each step it takes along that path.

    ▶ Your judgment is your contribution to the process of choosing the company's future.

    ▶ The decisions you make are an expression of your values. Put yourself in a place and frame of mind in which the values expressed by your decisions—strength and optimism—are values you want to represent you.

    ▶ Be comfortable choosing and moving on.

14. **Implementation**

    Make it happen.

    ▸ Execution is where your plan becomes a reality and where the most value is created.

    ▸ Something will go wrong.

    ▸ You must be clear—by what you say and how you act—that you expect and welcome both good news and bad news.

    ▸ Success requires a continuous Create the Future Thinking cycle where you Ask, Discover, Learn, and Decide.

APPENDIX B

TEAM EXERCISES AND WORK PRODUCTS

GETTING STARTED

Is this the book for you? How to create the future. Chapter summaries.

Exercise: *None*

PART ONE: PREPARE THE COMPANY AND YOURSELF

1. **Create the Future Thinking**

   Ask, discover, learn, and decide.

   Exercises: *None*

2. **Your Zone of Leadership**

   You are not the company. Choose your own future.

   Exercise 2-1: *My Job Today*

EXERCISE WORK PRODUCT

- My Job Today Profile identifying your special strengths and weaknesses and your job's impact on your personal and family life

   Exercise 2-2: *Strengths and Passions*

EXERCISE WORK PRODUCTS

- My Strengths
- My Passions

- My Motivations in terms of success and achievement

Exercise 2-3: *Zone of Leadership*

EXERCISE WORK PRODUCTS
- Definition of your Zone of Leadership
- Profile of your ideal Zone of Leadership Job

3. The Leader's Role

Decision Maker, Leader of the Company, and Team Leader.

Exercise 3-1: *Your Motives for Using CTF*

EXERCISE WORK PRODUCTS
- Statement of your Motivation for using CTF and your Goals for the work
- Leader's Initial Decisions to Be Made Statement

Exercise 3-2: *Your Leadership Statement*

EXERCISE WORK PRODUCTS
- The Problem—The Leader's Statement
- Success—The Leader's Statement
- Why You Should Care—Elevator Pitch for the company and CTF

4. Engage the Team

Decision Makers and trusted advisors create the future together.

Exercise 4-1: *CTF Team Objectives for Its Work*

EXERCISE WORK PRODUCTS
- Team Success Statement of goals for its contribution to the CTF work
- Summary of common themes of individual member's goals for their participation on the CTF Team

PART TWO: DEFINE THE CHALLENGE

5. **Define the Challenge**

    Solve the right problem.

    Exercise 5-1: *The Challenge*

    EXERCISE WORK PRODUCT
    - Challenge Statement defining the opportunity or threat facing the company and driving the CTF work

PART THREE: IMAGINE SUCCESS

6. **Success, Goals, and Values**

    What success looks like.

    Exercise 6-1: *Success—Aspiration and Strategy*

    EXERCISE WORK PRODUCTS
    - Success Statement qualitatively describing success and the permissions and constraints on what the organization can and cannot do to achieve success
    - A Vision Statement describing the challenge and profiling a vision of success

    Exercise 6-2: *Success as an Expression of Values*

    EXERCISE WORK PRODUCTS
    - A Values Statement describing values to be considered when the preferred Future Choice is selected
    - Addition of the Values Statement to the Success Statement and the Vision Statement

    Exercise 6-3: *Goals—Operational Targets*

EXERCISE WORK PRODUCT
- Operational Goals Statement including levels of performance and the time frame for achieving success

PART FOUR: CREATE OPTIONS

7. Paths to Success
Different ways to solve the problem.

Exercise 7-1: *Categories of Future Choices*

EXERCISE WORK PRODUCTS
- Categories of Future Choices for achieving the company's goals
- No-Go Categories—Initiatives not to be considered

8. Choices for the Future
Create options for the path to success.

Exercise 8-1: *All Ideas Are Good Ideas*

EXERCISE WORK PRODUCTS
- Long List of Future Choices for achieving the company's goals
- No-Go Options not to be considered further

Exercise 8-2: *Choices for the Future*

EXERCISE WORK PRODUCT
- Choices for the Future—Six or fewer options for achieving the organization's goals

Exercise 8-3: *Benefits of the Future Choices*

EXERCISE WORK PRODUCT
- Future Choices Benefits Matrix—A summary of the primary benefits of each Future Choice

PART FIVE: EVALUATE BARRIERS TO SUCCESS

9. **Execution Barriers**

    Getting there from here.

    Exercise 9-1: *What Must Go Right?—Essential Requirements for Success*

    EXERCISE WORK PRODUCTS

    ▸ Requirements for Success Matrix for each Future Choice showing important elements of the execution plan with a high level of success uncertainty

    ▸ List of Essential Requirements for Success identifying "must go right" elements of each Future Choice's implementation plan with a high level of success uncertainty separated into internal and external categories

    Exercise 9-2: *What Might Go Wrong?—Company Operations Today*

    EXERCISE WORK PRODUCT

    ▸ List of the Most Important Execution Risks for each Future Choice, including a description of the company's relevant current capabilities

    Exercise 9-3: *What Will Happen?—Success Prospects*

    EXERCISE WORK PRODUCTS

    ▸ Overcoming Execution Barriers Estimate displaying the estimated likelihood each execution barrier will be overcome

    ▸ Benefits and Barriers Profile summarizing the primary benefits and barriers of each Future Choice

10. **Key Assumptions**

    What you assume will happen and will not happen.

    Exercise 10-1: *Key Assumption Options*

EXERCISE WORK PRODUCTS
- ▸ Key Assumption List for each Choice for the Future
- ▸ Key Assumption Options listing alternative assumptions Deciders could make about future events and performance levels essential to the success of each Future Choice

PART SIX: CHOOSE THE FUTURE

11. Decision Agenda
What decisions must I make?

Exercise 11-1: *Decision Agenda*

EXERCISE WORK PRODUCTS
- ▸ Decision Agenda including a Decision Tree and a list of the Decisions to Be Made
- ▸ Decision Preparations List—Special preparation prior to decision meetings

12. Prepare to Choose
The "meaning" of your decision.

Exercise 12-1: *What Have We Learned? Do We Need to Know More?*

EXERCISE WORK PRODUCTS
- ▸ What We Learned about the Problem and the Choices for the Future
- ▸ Information to be gathered or experiments to be run to reduce risk, if any

Exercise 12-2: *Success, Risk, and Values Profile*

EXERCISE WORK PRODUCT
- ▸ Success, Risk, and Values Profile of each Choice for the Future

Exercise 12-3: *Key Assumptions—Team Recommendations*

EXERCISE WORK PRODUCT

> Key Assumptions—Team Recommendations

Exercise 12-4: *Choosing the Future—Team Recommendations*

EXERCISE WORK PRODUCT

> Choices for the Future—Team Rankings

13. **Choose the Future**

    Decide.

    Exercise 13-1: *Key Assumptions by Decision Makers*

EXERCISE WORK PRODUCTS

> Decision Agenda—Final Version
>
> Choices for the Future—Final Description
>
> Key Assumptions—Decision Maker Assumptions

Exercise 13-2: *Characterize the Choices for the Future*

EXERCISE WORK PRODUCTS

> Decision Maker characterization of their "ideal" Future Choice SRV Profile and of the Future Choices under consideration
>
> Decision Maker assessment of the impact the Choices will have on important constituents
>
> Primary drivers of the Decision Makers' selection of a Future Choice

Exercise 13-3: *Choose the Future*

EXERCISE WORK PRODUCT

> Choice for the Future—Decision Maker selection

14. Implementation

Make it happen.

`Exercise: *None*

ACKNOWLEDGMENTS

How I Wrote This Book

In 2018, I gave myself permission to go offline for several weeks to visit Barcelona and Morocco. In Morocco, I haggled over the price of a Berber carpet in the Marrakech Kasbah, rode a camel in the desert, and had dinner at Rick's Café in Casablanca. My parents named me after Humphrey Bogart's character in the movie *Casablanca*.

Exploring Barcelona and Morocco gave me time to think about what I have learned working with leaders, professors, coaches, and advisors.

I'd written and spoken about leadership for many years. As a management consultant, I advised large companies and government agencies on best management practices. Some people ask whether I have written a book about leadership. I'd written many book-length reports that clients paid big fees to have me and my teams prepare. But you cannot buy these reports in the business or leadership section of the bookstore or download them to Kindle.

My thoughts kept going back to the idea that clients usually did not hire me to solve a mystery that was beyond their ability to solve. Most often, they were trying to decide where to take their organization and needed help preparing and then making the decision.

Most, even all, of the information and insights needed to make the decision were available, but they did not have time or know-how to compile the information in a format relevant to choosing the path forward. They also needed help creating a process for deciding where to take the company.

While sitting at a rooftop café in Casablanca, I turned the placemat over and wrote *Create the Future*—the title of this book. Below the title, I wrote several concepts, including "break away from the demands of the moment to create the future."

Starting to write the book was the next challenge. I put a stake in the ground by signing up for a business book writer's workshop hosted by Sheila

Heen and Doug Stone. While working at Harvard Law School's Program on Negotiation, Sheila and Doug somehow found time to write *Difficult Conversations* and *Thanks for the Feedback*. They shared their experience with writers from around the world.

Before coming to the workshop in Newport, Rhode Island, my homework assignment was to write a one-page summary of what my book was "about"—who it is for, what problem it solves, why it is important, and what a reader gets from it. Writing that one page was my first step in writing this book. Doug and Sheila pushed me from having an idea for a book to starting to write the book.

I started writing with a structured consultant's approach. I had the title, capturing the book's basic idea. A chapter outline came next. I outlined the content for each chapter and listed the key points I wanted to make. If I were in my consultant's role, I would have assigned each chapter to a consulting team member to begin their research. I assigned all chapters to myself and started writing, beginning with the Introduction.

I asked colleagues who are experienced business leaders if they would join a review committee for the book. After writing each chapter, I asked the review committee for comments and suggestions. No editing. I only wanted their feedback on content and ideas. Each reviewer had a different point of view. Taken together, their comments strengthened one chapter after another.

Beginning early in the morning, I wrote each chapter in sequence and incorporated the review committee's comments. I then revised the book as a whole to connect the chapters with each other. After months of work, I had a completed book sitting on my desk in a three-ring binder. I thought I was finished or close to being finished. I was ready to find a publisher.

Before talking to potential publishers, I had questions about the book's overall organization. For example, where should examples of companies using the Create the Future methodology go in the chapter flow? I networked around, asking for recommendations for someone to look at my "about ready to be published book" who could help me with this last tweaking of the chapter organization.

Lucky break! A mutual friend introduced me to Merrill Meadow. Merrill had worked with and written about Howard Stevenson and other faculty at Harvard Business School. Merrill agreed to look at the book and give me suggestions and feedback.

Merrill came back to me and reported that, in his view, my book was "a good first draft." First draft? I thought I had given Merrill a close-to-being-finished, almost-ready-to-be-published book.

Merrill thought he was giving me good news. "A good first draft!" I am accustomed to the cannon firing when we sail across the finish line. Now what? Merrill and I discussed whether we should work together and, if so, how that would work. We agreed to work on a redraft of the book's introduction and see how that went.

Merrill started by throwing my Introduction into the circular file—too much about getting ready to read the book and too little about what the book is about. Merrill drafted a new seven-page introduction called "Getting Started." I tossed out Merrill's text and wrote, starting from scratch, a first draft of the introductory chapter, "Getting Started." We haggled over drafts three, four, and five until we were both satisfied.

Working together, we were doing more than writing a chapter of the book. Merrill taught me how to take the content I had written and turn it into focused and concise text. I then revised the other chapters with a more focused frame of mind. I could not have completed this book to the quality it is without Merrill Meadow's patience and generous help and guidance.

Thanks to Those Who Helped Me Create the Future

Those rare individuals who create and build successful companies have unreasonable confidence in their own vision and ability to succeed. Many tell them they are wrong and will not be successful, but they press on, driven by their own strength and belief in what they are doing.

Belief in yourself and your vision is necessary for success, but those qualities alone will not take your enterprise to a high level of achievement. You must also be open to learning from your mistakes, learning from others, and letting other team members and collaborators contribute in their areas of excellence.

The same principles apply to writing a book. Writing is a lonely process and also a collaborative process. I wrote the early drafts of this book alone in my office, mostly during the COVID-19 lockdown. I am not sure I would have finished the book if COVID-19 had not separated me from colleagues and friends for so long.

Many colleagues helped me take this book from a rough draft to a "good first draft" and then to the finished book you are reading. My chapter-by-chapter review committee included Regina Flynn, Mike McNulty, Scott Lewis, Steve Herman, and Josie DeMaso. Others helped, but these friends were on board for the whole trip.

Lucinda O'Neill was the creative genius responsible for the book's design and logo. Lucinda took the words on a black-and-white piece of paper and brought them to life visually.

I interviewed graphic designers across the globe, searching for someone to portray leadership-team whiteboard exercises. Poppy Rahayu lives in Indonesia. You will see Poppy's simple and compelling whiteboard illustrations in every chapter.

I spoke with many book publishers while learning the complicated story of book publishing options. I got to know Naren Aryal, CEO of Amplify Publishing Group, and decided to partner with Amplify. I wanted a publisher large enough to bring the book to the market but small enough to care about this book's success. I am grateful for Naren's counsel on how to take the book to the public and to Brandon Coward, publishing project manager, and his team at Amplify for getting the book into bookstores.

Two truths about writing a book: I could not have written a book of this quality without the support of many friends, colleagues, and professional teammates. And I only really knew what this book was about after I had written it. Thank you all.

ABOUT THE AUTHOR

Rick Williams is an internationally published author. He is a frequent speaker and writer on best practices for leadership and decision-making.

Williams began his career as a physicist developing space- and defense-related systems. After Harvard Business School, Williams joined the global consulting firm Arthur D. Little, Inc., where he worked on business strategy and acquisitions and the economic and strategic impact of government policy and regulations on a broad spectrum of industries. He then founded and served as CEO of The Equity Company, an award-winning real estate investment and development firm.

Williams's recent work includes serving on the board of directors of technology companies. He has served as board chairman of a medical device company and a bank/venture capital firm. He has also served on the national board for the Private Directors Association and as president of the Harvard Business School Association of Boston and other nonprofit boards. Williams is an honors physics graduate of the University of Pennsylvania, a winning sailboat racer, and an avid photographer.